HYBRID MEDIA EVENTS

The *Charlie Hebdo* Attacks and the
Global Circulation of Terrorist Violence

HYBRID MEDIA EVENTS

The *Charlie Hebdo* Attacks and the Global Circulation of Terrorist Violence

BY

JOHANNA SUMIALA
University of Helsinki, Helsinki, Finland

KATJA VALASKIVI
University of Tampere, Tampere, Finland

MINTTU TIKKA
University of Helsinki, Helsinki, Finland

JUKKA HUHTAMÄKI
Tampere University of Technology, Tampere, Finland

United Kingdom – North America – Japan – India – Malaysia – China

Emerald Publishing Limited
Howard House, Wagon Lane, Bingley BD16 1WA, UK

First edition 2018

Reprints and permissions service
Contact: permissions@emeraldinsight.com

British Library Cataloguing in Publication Data
A catalogue record for this book is available from the British Library

ISBN: 978-1-78714-852-9 (Print)
ISBN: 978-1-78714-851-2 (Online)
ISBN: 978-1-78743-916-0 (Epub)
ISBN: 978-1-78754-913-5 (Paperback)

Printed and bound by CPI Group (UK) Ltd, Croydon, CR0 4YY

ISOQAR certified
Management System,
awarded to Emerald
for adherence to
Environmental
standard
ISO 14001:2004.

Certificate Number 1985
ISO 14001

INVESTOR IN PEOPLE

Contents

List of Figures   *ix*

List of Tables   *xi*

List of Photographs   *xiii*

About the Authors   *xv*

Preface   *xvii*

Chapter 1   What Are Hybrid Media Events of Terrorist Violence?   *1*
1.1.   Why Do the *Charlie Hebdo* Attacks Matter?   *1*
1.2.   Towards Interdisciplinary Analysis of Media and Terrorism   *4*
       1.2.1.   Hybrid   *5*
       1.2.2.   Media Event   *9*
1.3.   On the Hybridization of Media Events   *13*
1.4.   The Five Elements of Hybrid Media Events   *16*
       1.4.1.   Actors   *17*
       1.4.2.   Affordance   *18*
       1.4.3.   Attention   *19*
       1.4.4.   Affect   *20*
       1.4.5.   Acceleration   *20*
1.5.   Analysing Hybrid Media Events on Twitter and Beyond   *21*
       1.5.1.   Three Empirical Phases   *23*
1.6.   Structure of the Book   *26*

Chapter 2   Creating a Media Event   *29*
2.1.   Many Beginnings   *29*
2.2.   *Charlie Hebdo* — A 'Bête et Méchant' Newspaper   *30*
2.3.   Remediation in Digital Media — Shootings Go Viral   *35*
2.4.   Mythologization of the Victims   *37*
       2.4.1.   News Coverage and Global Mourning   *37*
       2.4.2.   The Manhunt Continues   *40*
       2.4.3.   Who Counts as a Victim?   *41*

2.5. Condensation of Meaning(s)   *43*
  2.5.1. The World Political Elites Demonstrate
    Solidarity   *43*
  2.5.2. Counter-narratives Challenge the Main Storyline *45*
  2.5.3. 'Huge Show of Solidarity in Paris against
    Terrorism'   *49*
2.6. After the 'Je Suis Charlie' Momentum   *51*

Chapter 3 Actors and Affordances   *57*
3.1. Accounts and Hashtags   *59*
3.2. The Anatomy of the *Charlie Hebdo* Attacks on Twitter   *60*
  3.2.1. Actors   *63*
  3.2.2. Dynamics   *65*
3.3. Tracing #JeSuisKouachi: Affordances of Hashtags   *72*
3.4. Hybrid Media Events Amplify Themselves   *75*

Chapter 4 Attention   *77*
4.1. Ahmed Merabet's Death Goes Viral   *77*
4.2. The Media Makes Merabet an Ideal Victim   *80*
4.3. Controversy over the Video   *81*
4.4. 'Je Suis Ahmed' as a Symbol of Public Solidarity   *83*
4.5. Politicizing the Muslim Body   *86*
4.6. Accumulation and Circulation of Attention   *87*

Chapter 5 Affect   *89*
5.1. Rituals Intensify the Sense of Solidarity in Media   *91*
5.2. 'Je Suis Charlie' in Social Media   *95*
5.3. Funerals   *96*
5.4. Narratives Opposed to 'Je Suis Charlie' Solidarity   *99*
5.5. Circulation of Fear Addresses Diverse Audiences   *102*
5.6. Hybridization and Ritual Practices   *104*

Chapter 6 Liveness and Acceleration of Circulation   *107*
6.1. Hostage Situation in Dammartin-en-Goële   *108*
6.2. The Kosher Market Siege   *113*
  6.2.1. Live Broadcasting Puts Hostages in Danger   *116*
6.3. The Aftermath   *116*
6.4. Acceleration of Circulation in a Hybrid Media Event   *119*

Chapter 7 ***Charlie Hebdo* and the Circulation of Terrorist**
    Violence in a Hybrid Media Event *123*
7.1. Circulation Connects Key Elements *126*
7.2. Towards a Discussion of the Social and Ethical
      Dimensions of Hybrid Media Events *127*
7.3. What Can Be Done? *130*

References *135*

Index *149*

List of Figures

Chapter 2

Figure 2.1. Number of Hashtags #JeSuisCharlie,
#JeNeSuisPasCharlie and #JeSuisAhmed on Twitter
during the First 10 Days after the Attacks 39

Chapter 3

Figure 3.1. Top 20 Most Used Hashtags in Twitter Messages
Posted on the *Charlie Hebdo* Attacks 62

Figure 3.2. Scatter Plot of the Relationship between Number of
Twitter Users' Followers and the Numbers of Retweets
They Received 67

Figure 3.3. Network Visualization of the Most Authoritative
Actors in the Twitter Data 69

List of Tables

Chapter 3

Table 3.1.   Top 20 Users with the Largest Number of
Retweets   64

Table 3.2.   How Twitter Actors Mention Twitter
in Their Tweets   71

List of Photographs

Chapter 2

Place de la République, 11 January. Image by Olivier Ortelpa,
Creative Commons Flickr 50

Chapter 4

Ahmed Merabet on News Covers. 79

About the Authors

Johanna Sumiala, PhD, is Associate Professor of Religion and the Digital World at the Faculty of Theology, University of Helsinki. She is an expert in the fields of media sociology and media anthropology, digital ethnography and visual culture. She has recently published articles on mediatized violence and ritualized (online) communication, and she is the author of the book *Media and Ritual: Death, Community and Everyday Life* (2013).

Katja Valaskivi, Associate Professor (Docent), is the Research Director of Tampere Research Centre for Journalism, Media and Communication (COMET) and Vice Dean of the Faculty of Communication Sciences (COMS) at the University of Tampere, Finland. She is a media scholar, who has published widely in the issues of media and the nation, nation branding and circulation in media society. The title of her most recent book is *Cool Nations: Media and the Social Imaginary of the Branded Country* (2016).

Minttu Tikka is a PhD Candidate at the Department of Social Research/Media and Communication Studies, University of Helsinki. She is interested in developing methods for studying internet and social media. She has published issues of crises, terrorism and digital media, YouTube and news and digital ethnography.

Jukka Huhtamäki is a Postdoctoral Researcher at Laboratory of Industrial and Information Management, Tampere University of Technology, and at Tampere Research Centre for Journalism, Media and Communication (COMET), Finland. He is also a Co-founder of Innovation Ecosystems Network. He is developing methodology for extracting, analysing and visualizing heterogeneous data for system-level insights on various kinds of socio-technical phenomenon.

Preface

This book has many beginnings, but one stands out above all others: the attack on the *Charlie Hebdo* offices in Paris on 7 January 2015. When news about the shootings began to pour into our social media feeds, we decided straightaway to start compiling research data. We followed the messaging on Twitter and Facebook, we tracked Finnish and international news sources and we witnessed the appearance of the #JeSuisCharlie hashtag.

Charlie Hebdo was not a chance selection, nor were we interested in the event simply because of the huge attention it attracted. We had already been researching attention for many years, exploring the creation and circulation of attention in a changed media environment: we wanted to understand how things, notions, ideologies and values come into being and how they exercise an impact and influence on the media through circulation. We had also studied the ways in which different actors participate in and the roles they had in these circulation processes. Furthermore, we shared an interest in the different ways that religion is thematized in the media. For years, Johanna had followed and studied violent media events, while Katja's research interest was focused on the global media circulation of different phenomena. Most of this work was grounded in an ethnographic approach, but in this case we wanted to expand and diversify our methodological toolkit. Our ambitious plan, initially, was to collect all the data from all possible sources, to study circulation patterns from one platform to another and to develop methods that combine an ethnographic approach with computational methods. However, we had neither the funding nor the resources to do this.

We, therefore, decided we should assemble a team, start to write funding applications and narrow our perspective. We were joined by Jukka Huhtamäki from Tampere University of Technology, who we had worked with before at the Tampere Research Centre for Journalism, Media and Communication COMET; and by Minttu Tikka, with whom Johanna had collaborated for many years. Throughout the project all of us on the team have shared a common commitment to better understand the changes happening in the media environment and the relationship between media and society in general — and to develop the tools and research methods we need to achieve this understanding. This team effort is still ongoing.

Thankfully the funding we needed came very quickly. First, we secured a grant from the Helsingin Sanomat Foundation in 2015, mainly for our project 'Je suis Charlie — The symbolic battle and struggle over attention', which was focused on studying the media attention surrounding the attack on the *Charlie Hebdo* newspaper. Later, in 2017, the Academy of Finland awarded us funding for a project dealing with the relationship between the media and terrorism more generally. This ongoing project is called 'Hybrid Terrorizing: Developing a New Model for the Study of Global Media Events of Terrorist Violence (HYTE)'.[1]

However, even though we had the funding in place, it was not until six months after the events in Paris that we could start compiling the research data. As it turned out, data collection and data administration became a long-drawn-out rigmarole that went on for almost three years. Once we get the chance, we will report on this in greater detail. Based on what we have heard, colleagues in other countries seem to have very similar problems when it comes to accessing and administering large datasets. The problem is particularly difficult in cases where we have to rely for data on commercial service providers — which we do in order to gain access to social media datasets.

Because we had problems gaining access to historical data and because the volume of data was so huge, we chose to concentrate on messages circulating in Twitter. The dataset was obtained from a company called Pulsar, which specializes in mining and collecting data from different social media platforms. The decision to use Twitter data proved to be a good one, in that Twitter is very much the epitome of the hybrid media environment: it has large amounts of circulating data that are produced in different ways and organized by hashtags. Our decision was driven by practical considerations, even though we were aware that Twitter attracts disproportionate research attention compared to its user numbers. The reason for this lies in Twitter's technological design, which allows for easy data collection and data transfer in different formats. As well as taking advantage of these technological features, we have collected supplementary data from international online news providers, and to a minor extent from Facebook and YouTube.

The idea for this book was born in 2016, shortly after we had hosted the Tampere 'Workshop on Media, Event and Social Theory —

---

[1]Grants number 308850 (Valaskivi) and 308854 (Sumiala).

Transnational Challenges for Analysis'. Feedback from our first project's advisory board and inspiring dialogue with the invited workshop speakers made us realize that we had tapped into a subject that might well have the makings of a book. We wish to thank the members of the advisory board of 'Je suis Charlie — The symbolic battle and struggle over attention': Marwan Kraidy, Gawan Titley, Tuomas Martikainen, Anna Roosvall and Farida Vis for inspiring discussions, feedback and support. In addition, we wish to thank the other workshop speakers: Sabina Mihelj, Andreas Hepp, Peter Hervik, Chris Rojek, Anu Kantola, Risto Kunelius and Nico Carpentier. Nick Couldry had to cancel his attendance at the workshop, but he has always been a constant source of support and help. We'd also like to thank other colleagues who have commented on our work at several conferences, including the members of the ECREA temporary working group on media and religion round-table discussion 'Media, Religion and Conflict — Contemporary European Perspectives' in Prague in 2016.

Our thanks also go to Media and Communication Studies at the University of Helsinki; the Faculty of Communication Sciences at the University of Tampere and its predecessors; the Tampere Research Centre for Journalism, Media and Communication COMET; Tampere University of Technology; all our colleagues at these institutions for their support and inspiring discussions; the Nordic Network on Media and Religion and its annual retreat-like gatherings in Sigtuna, Sweden; and the Finnish Institute in Rome (Villa Lante), where Katja had the opportunity to concentrate on full-time writing in March 2017. Thanks also to David Kivinen, Anu Harju and Paula Kallio for their assistance in finalizing the manuscript. We are indebted to our editors at Emerald, Jen McCall and Rachel Ward, whose friendly support and encouragement got us through the final hectic stages of writing. And lastly and most importantly, we owe a special thanks to our family members for their patience and love — and for being there.

Johanna Sumiala
Katja Valaskivi
Minttu Tikka
Jukka Huhtamäki
Editors

Chapter 1

What Are Hybrid Media Events of Terrorist Violence?

1.1. Why Do the *Charlie Hebdo* Attacks Matter?

On 7 January 2015, Paris and the rest of the Western world was holding its breath, following every movement in a manhunt launched after a terrorist attack on the French satirical newspaper *Charlie Hebdo*. Twelve people had been killed at the newspaper's offices. The terror attack that was carried out by the Kouachi brothers, who were later shot and killed in a police raid, received massive media interest and sparked an instant global media event. The news circulated in the local, national and international news media and on social networking sites. Symbols of public mourning and messages of solidarity, but also of fear, hate and anger, travelled at high speed from one actor and media platform to another (see also Zagato, 2015; Sumiala, 2017).

While the global media was following and reporting the unfolding events, it also felt the need to try to make sense of what was happening, to offer some explanation. On 8 January, the American internet news service Kicker — which promises to 'explain top stories in a super help-ful, super engaging, super empowering way' — provided a five-point list under the title '5 Reasons Why the *Charlie Hebdo* Massacre in France Matters to Everyone in the Free World'. These reasons were (Kicker, 2015)[1]:

1. Free speech is a human right, but some intensely dispute that.
2. It forces us to think about the possible limits of free speech.
3. There is a connection between extremist Islam and violence as a retaliation tactic.
4. This is part of a string of similar attacks.
5. It might feed anti-immigrant feelings in Europe.

---

[1]http://gokicker.com/about/ (Retrieved 14 March 2017).

Each of these reasons was illustrated with numerous examples of texts, images and memes that circulated in the social media in the aftermath of the *Charlie Hebdo* attacks. The explanations and their illustrations were focused on the political and social implications of the attacks. At the same time, the piece was a media text that circulated other media texts, a representation referring to other representations in an attempt to illustrate what had happened and why that had significance. Although perhaps unusually reflexive, the piece was otherwise just another addition to an endless stream of media texts that were trying to make sense of the media event and its consequences. As such it was closely involved in the reproduction and circulation of the event, although it failed to recognize its own role in the causation and interpretation of the event. Furthermore, the piece was grounded in a framework where the world is seen as being divided into the Free World and the rest, a threatening place that questions the values of what it means to be 'free'.

In this book, we set out to explore how the media are involved and intertwined with a global event of terrorist violence, and to identify which dimensions of the hybrid media environment play a part in the ensuing social imaginaries and symbolic battles. As a first step in this effort, the Kicker example above serves to illustrate just how involved and intertwined the media are, not only in the *Charlie Hebdo* attacks, but in the process of making sense of the event.

In the hybrid media system (Chadwick, 2013), the practices of professional, journalistic and social media are closely interwoven. Lines between production and consumption are blurred, and meanings are formed in an endless circulation of texts, visuals and meanings. The internet revenue model is based on the attention economy (Davenport & Beck, 2001; Goldhaber, 1997; see also Webster, 2014), that is the success of professional media companies depends on the number of clicks and shares their stories receive. Algorithms are also used to determine which types of contents are circulated to particular audiences. This circulation takes place in the marketplace of attention (Webster, 2014), where audiences are active in creating and circulating content, but at the same time depend more and more on what social media platforms and their algorithms curate for their feed.

The effectiveness of terrorist attacks has always depended on the attention they manage to attract, and the amount of collective fear they manage to instil. Terrorism cannot be separated from communication, for without communication of terrorists' messages the effect of terrorism would be significantly reduced (Archetti, 2012; Klopfenstein, 2007). Contemporary terrorism makes skilful use of the hybrid media environment in seeking attention. At the same time, the media manifold (Couldry, 2012; Couldry & Hepp, 2016) is so complex that no individual actor — terrorists included — can control circulation in a hybrid media event (Sumiala, Tikka, & Valaskivi, 2019; Sumiala, Tikka, Huhtamäki, & Valaskivi, 2016; Vaccari, Chadwick, & O'Loughlin, 2015).

In this book, we argue that the *Charlie Hebdo* attacks need to be understood as a global media event in a string of terrorist incidents since 9/11. In the past 15 years or so since the attacks on the World Trade Center, the media environment has changed significantly, as have ways of conceptualizing terrorism in association with radical Islam (Nacos, 2016). The 9/11 attacks and their aftermath have resulted in a world where an ambiguous fear of Muslim terrorism is used as political leverage to restrict and curtail citizens' rights through surveillance and — paradoxically — constraints on freedom of speech (Cottle, 2006b). The aim of terrorism, which is to seek attention and instil fear, has not changed, and terrorism has — unfortunately — been quite successful in feeding into fear (Archetti, 2012). In other words, 9/11 provided a traumatic context for all those following violent acts of terror. Since then, the cultural imaginary of terrorism has mainly been framed in terms of Islam.

The circulation of affect makes a metonymic connection (Ahmed, 2004a, 2004b) between Islam and terrorism. That connection is now so strong that the initial reaction to any and every violent incident is to suspect Islamist terrorism (Nacos, 2016; see also Said, 1981/1997). It is not an uncommon observation that when the perpetrator is white and indigenous, the search for explanations focuses on individual personality traits and personal history, from upbringing and media usage to issues of mental health. But when the perpetrator is thought to be 'an outsider', it seems that references to cultural background and religion are explanations enough; there is no need to address individual reasons (cf. Khiabany & Williamson, 2012). For instance, in the wake of the Utøya massacre in Norway in 2011, politicians and the media in Northern Europe were quick to make comments that the perpetrator must be a Muslim. When it turned out that Anders Breivik was blond and blue-eyed and held extreme right political sympathies, the explanations shifted to his troubled childhood, absent father, bullying at school and, finally, distorted relationship with his mother (cf. Borchgrevink, 2013). By contrast, the Kouachi brothers, who were born in France and who grew up in deprived Parisian suburbs, were portrayed not as 'boys of our own' who had gone astray, but as external Muslim terrorists who had come into French society from the outside to carry out their cowardly attacks. In this way both Islam and the attackers were framed as outsiders to France, and to the West in general (Todd, 2015).

In this book, we argue that contemporary media events of terrorist violence play out in the ways they do because of the contemporary hybrid media environment. We do not mean to suggest that technological advances are the actual cause of these events, but rather that the practices, range and reach of consequences and circulated social imaginaries of a media event are always ingrained in the technologies available, and so provide particular affordances, narratives, modes of communication, genres and repertoires. The whole of our contemporary 'social world is fundamentally interwoven with media' (Couldry & Hepp, 2016, p. 16).

Our media environment today is largely the outcome of a process of technological development geared to creating new business opportunities through the internet. This (technological) business focus has had side-effects that are felt in societies throughout the world. These side-effects include the creation of polarizing 'bubbles' that are enhanced by social media algorithms, and those bubbles make possible the fabrication and spreading of lies and rumours for economic and political gain, as well as some features of datafication that contribute to increasing inequality (cf. Pariser, 2011). Methods of branding, propaganda and promotion are used by various actors, including terrorists. These tendencies obviously tie in with wider socio-historical, economic and political developments, and the aftermath of neoliberal global capitalism. In this book, however, we apply the lens of the media event.

1.2. Towards Interdisciplinary Analysis of Media and Terrorism

Contemporary terrorist violence is a complicated and shifting area of study and discussion that is extensively covered in a range of disciplines in the social and political sciences (see, e.g., Kepel, 2017; Roy, 2016). There is also a body of literature that addresses the role of (journalistic) media in terrorism (see, e.g., Altheide, 1987; Kavoori & Fraley, 2006). The role of media in terrorism has attracted academic research interest for decades. Much of this work has focused on the contents, meanings and frames of (journalistic) media in their coverage of terrorism, be it in newspapers or television (for more on the study of media and terrorism, see, e.g., Archetti, 2012; Nacos, 2016).

The aim of this book is to advance our understanding of the relationship between media and terrorism in the contemporary hybrid media environment where hybrid media events escalate, circulate and cumulate. Our approach is inspired by several intellectual sources, including media anthropology, international communication and political communication, and recent discussions on media and social theory. We hope to be able to produce a map of the territory of hybrid media events of terrorist violence and provide new insights into the dynamics of the present media environment, which would help people and societies better comprehend what is at stake in these conflicts rather than escalate them.

Our analysis of the unfolding of the *Charlie Hebdo* attacks as a hybrid media event applies an approach that views media events as ruptures big enough in the ordinary flow of occurrences to create new meanings. In this process, we revisit some of the earlier historical, philosophical and sociological theorizing on events and bring them into a new type of dialogue with the line of media events research first initiated by Daniel Dayan and Elihu Katz in 1992. In this book, we argue for the necessity of looking more carefully into the interplay between the media environment and the dynamics of global imagination activated in a given context. We claim that understanding the hybridization of the present media environment is essential in order to grasp what is happening in today's media events of terror and the global narratives that are told in those media-saturated events in the present digital age. But first, in order to set the framework for this book, we introduce and elaborate our understanding of two key concepts central to our analysis: *hybrid* and media event.

1.2.1. Hybrid

Although the concept of hybrid is enjoying current popularity in academic discourse, with numerous scholars in different fields expounding their ideas in relation to hybrid (see, e.g., AlSayyad, 2001; Smith & Leavy, 2009; Whatmore, 2002), the concept goes back quite some time. Roman statesman and philosopher Pliny the Elder (AD 79) used the concept to describe bizarre creatures from far and exotic lands, part animal and part-human (Chadwick, 2013, p. 8).

In the seventeenth century, the word was adopted to refer to mixed racial inheritance. At around the same time, it also assumed a more metaphorical meaning, referring to things that have different origins, or heterogeneous sources. In biological contexts, the concept is still used today to refer to cross-breeds between plants or animals; in computer technology to describe mixtures of digital and analogue technologies and in the automative industry to refer to cars that run on more than one source of power. All in all, 'hybridity alerts us to the unusual things that happen when distinct entities come together to create something new that nevertheless has continuities with the old' (Chadwick, 2013, p. 9). In social sciences, hybridity is an interdisciplinary trend that cuts across several fields. In organizational studies research, for instance, there is growing interest in 'hybrid organizations' (Billis, 2010). Andrew Chadwick notes that hybridity can be seen as 'something like an ontology', a theoretical disposition providing us with the opportunity to ask and answer new kinds of questions about 'the nature of contemporary society'.

But the concept of hybridity does have its problems. Analysing hybridity is inherently difficult, as it implies the existence of pure baseline forms, before they are mixed and blended, and historically it has proved hard to find such forms. Following Edward Said, Marwan Kraidy refers to the concept of hybridity as 'contrapuntal', which he says is 'well suited for understanding the relational aspects of hybridity because it stresses the formative role of exchanges between participating entities' (Kraidy, 2005, p. 13).

Our aim in this book is to explore hybridity in the context of the contemporary media environment. To that end we have identified three writers — Marwan M. Kraidy (2005), Bruno Latour (1993) and Andrew Chadwick (2013) — whom we will be referring to in order to describe aspects of hybridity that can help us understand hybrid media events.[2]

Bruno Latour's idea of hybridity is twofold, or rather two sides of the same coin. On the one hand, he talks about how the distinction between nature and culture/society in modern Western thinking is counterintuitive and counterproductive; on the other hand, he emphasizes the hybridity between human and non-human actors. In his famous book-length essay *We Have Never Been Modern* (1993), he calls for an anthropological approach to Western societies that sees beyond the distinctions between institutions in the modern West. Latour uses the media, and newspapers in particular, as an example of compartmentalization. His essay begins with a description of his wading through *Le Monde*, where the world is neatly separated into sections: science, politics, economy, law, religion, technology and fiction. Latour's critique is

---

[2]It is noteworthy that Chadwick's theory of hybridity draws heavily on the thinking of Kraidy.

focused not on the media, however, but on academic thinking. For him, the problem lies in different 'fiefdoms of criticism': epistemologists are all focused on facts and insist on the real; sociologists are obsessed with power and the collective and deconstructionalists are fixated on the constructed and discursive. His practical solution is the Actor Network Theory (ANT), which proposes to look at (hybrid) networks of actors, both human and non-human, in a seamless fabric of nature-culture — all actors that are at once real (like nature), narrated (like discourse) and collective (like society) (Latour, 1993, p. 6).

Marwan M. Kraidy (2005) takes a communicative perspective and discusses hybridity in the context of culture, international communication and media. Hybridity, he says, typically requires cross-cultural contact: it involves 'the fusion of distinct forms, styles, or identities that span across national or cultural boundaries'. This contact can assume the form of either movement of cultural commodities, such as media programmes or exchange through the media, or movement of people. Both involve the transfer of ideas and practices, giving way to hybridization. But Kraidy's approach extends beyond culture as he points out that present-day hybrid media are shaped by politico-economic considerations, in that 'the pervasiveness of hybridity in some ways reflects the growing synchronization of world markets' (Kraidy, 2005, p. 9). Furthermore, Kraidy notes that hybridity is fully compatible with globalization.

Both Latour and Kraidy place great weight on the question of culture. Latour (1993) talks about the relationship between the West and the non-West, while Kraidy criticizes the discursive, unhelpful division between 'the West' and 'the rest'. Latour insists that it is the West that has separated nature from society, and that by viewing the two on a (hybrid) nature-culture continuum it would be possible for the West to undo the division of cultures. He suggests that if the division between nature and culture is no longer seen as an epistemological question, then the West could also be viewed through the anthropologist's lens. This is very much taken for granted in contemporary anthropology, where it is just as ordinary and commonplace to study 'our own' societies as it is to explore 'the other'. In recent years, media ethnographical approaches have particularly contributed to this line of inquiry (see, e.g., Rothenbuhler & Coman, 2005). Yet the cultural and symbolic division between us and them has certainly not disappeared.

Andrew Chadwick's (2013) starting point is what Latour would call modernist: he works from the premise that hybridity is about blending institutional boundaries and roles. Chadwick is particularly interested in exploring the relationship between media (as in journalism) and politics. His approach derives from political communication, and he takes a special interest in elections. His analysis is firmly rooted in the Anglo-American context, and his concept of hybrid media system reflects this particular socio-geographic-historical context. In his own words, his aim is to 'provide an empirically informed interpretive account of key aspects of systemic change in the political communication environments of Britain and the United States', countries that have 'what are now best characterized as hybrid media systems' (Chadwick, 2013, p. 3). In this context, hybridity refers to the integrated roles that so-called older and newer media play in political communication in these two countries. Chadwick's focus is to study systemic characteristics, particularly with a view to seeing how the logics of older and newer media practices intertwine and how newer media practices interpenetrate the practices of both the older media and politics.

As we can see, then, the concept of hybridity has been used in different ways in relation to media and communication. The epistemological premises of the three approaches discussed above differ to some degree, which obviously presents a challenge for combining them and using them together. Having said that, there are also important similarities and points in common. All three writers acknowledge the presence of hybridity in culture, and the presence of hybridity across different domains of society.

But our aim and purpose here is to take inspiration from each of these three writers and to apply their theories in ways that are relevant to our case, that is to global hybrid media events of terrorist violence. From Latour, we adopt the idea of hybridity between human and non-human actors, the seamless fabric of nature-culture that is manifested in our contemporary media environment that intertwines technology, human action and discourses. Kraidy provides us guidance when we discuss power relations in global hybrid culture and in the world of international communication and media, and imbalances caused by overly simplified views of the relationship between 'the West' and 'the rest'. He also provides us with the tool of critical transculturalism, which allows us to focus on power in intercultural relations by integrating agency and structure into international communication analysis. Chadwick's empirically grounded idea of the hybridity of the media system helps us gain an analytical view of our empirical data, which consists of hybrid materials from both older and newer media outlets. Having said that, we step back from Chadwick's emphasis on old and new media logics and from the systemic approach, and use the concept of hybrid media environment instead of system. For us, environment more accurately reflects the kind of flexibility and openness that is necessary to understand the floating dynamics at play in today's hybrid media events of global violence. Furthermore, unlike Chadwick, we do not tie our discussion to a particular national media system, but take a wider view on media events.

1.2.2. Media Event

Events in human life have been the subject of theorizing by philosophers, historians, sociologists and social theorists alike (see, e.g., Abbott, 2001; Badiou, 2015; Deleuze, 1994; Sewell, 2005; Wagner-Pacifici, 2017). However, the first *theory* of media events was developed by communication scholars, Daniel Dayan and Elihu Katz, who had written about media events throughout the 1980s and in 1992 published *Media Events: The Live Broadcasting of History*. Their book has gained prominence not only in media and communication studies, but more generally in social science thinking about the interplay between media and public events in modern society.

Dayan and Katz's original idea was that a media event is a special genre that is powerful enough to interrupt the everyday media flow, bring the viewer into touch with society's central (sacred) values and invite the audience to participate in the event (Dayan & Katz, 1992, pp. 5–9). In their lexicon, media events have (a) their own grammar; (b) their own meaning structure (story form or script) and (c) their own practices characterized by live broadcasting: the interruption of daily media rhythms and routines, the scripting and advance preparation of the event, a huge audience (the 'whole world' is watching), social and normative expectations attached to viewing ('must see'), the ceremonial tone of media narration and the intention to connect people. As the story evolves and takes form, media events can be divided into 'conquests', 'contests' and 'coronations'.

Dayan and Katz's original work has a strong focus on *ceremoniality* and its power to promote social cohesion. Their subtitle — 'The Live Broadcasting of History' — points to the existence of a temporal aspect in a media event (cf. Sreberny, 2016; Zelizer, 2018). Dayan and Katz (1992) maintain that in many cases, the patterned story forms of a media event are closely intertwined and in live interaction with each other. This is to say that a media event can involve elements of more than one story form (e.g., the story form of 'contest' can also include elements of another story form, such as 'conquest'). Furthermore, the form of an event may change, transforming into another story form as the event unfolds (e.g., from conquest to coronation). It is also important to acknowledge that all these scripts are embedded in deeper symbolic meaning structures in a given culture (Dayan & Katz, 1992, pp. 28−29). Dayan and Katz indicate that the significance of media events lies in their ability to reach a larger audience than any event that requires physical presence. In so doing, they take the question of a media event pointing beyond itself to a new mediatized level. In their thinking, the audience itself is well aware of this as they follow the unfolding media event in different locations, which may be private, semi-public or public, local, national or transnational, and even global.

Since the publication of Dayan and Katz's book almost thirty years ago, media event theory has stimulated much debate among media and communication scholars, as well as has attracted recognition for its theoretical innovation (Hepp & Couldry, 2010, p. 2; see also Cottle, 2006a; Couldry, 2003; Couldry & Hepp, 2017; Dayan, 2010; Fiske, 1994; Hepp & Krotz, 2008; Katz & Liebes, 2007; Kyriakidou, 2008; Liebes, 1998; Nossek, 2008; Rothenbuhler, 1998; Scannell, 1995, 2001, 2017; Sreberny, 2016; Sumiala, 2013; Sumiala & Valaskivi, 2018; Zelizer, 2018). The main criticisms against Dayan and Katz's approach have concerned (1) the assumed ceremonial and integrative functions of media events, (2) the attempt to exclude any disruptive or traumatic events from the focus of their theory, (3) the strong focus on television and broadcasting and (4) the presentist tendency in media events, which freezes events in time (see also Sonnevend, 2016, p. 10).

Scholars in the critical tradition (see, e.g., Cottle, 2006a; Couldry, 2003, 2012) have argued that Dayan and Katz's initial account of media events assumed too straightforward a relationship between media coverage and audience endorsement, thereby obscuring the ideological construction of social order. Tamar Liebes together with Menahem Blondheim (Liebes, 1998; Liebes & Blondheim, 2005) has insisted that the theory of media events needs to expand towards disruptive events of terror and violence (see also Cottle, 2006a; Couldry, 2003; Fiske, 1994; Kellner, 2003; Kyriakidou, 2008; Rothenbuhler, 2010; Scannell, 1995, 2001). In addition, given the globalization of communication through the internet and social networking sites, critics have called for a re-contextualization of the explicit focus on TV and broadcasting (e.g., Hepp & Couldry, 2010). It has also been argued that the theory fails to reflect fully enough on the act of time in media events. It fails to explain how the narratives of and around media events change, endure or even fade over time (Sonnevend, 2016, p. 11).

Media historian Paddy Scannell (2014, p. 179) has contextualized the debate around media event theory and points out that Dayan and Katz 'knew full well that they were taking a very different stance to most if not all current academic orthodoxies'. Scannell argues that the core of the critical response was a dislike of the idea of public life as theatre. Referring to Dayan and Katz, Scannell (2014, p. 180) writes: 'They were at odds with all those, who one way or another, were dismissive of public life as theatre and television as its publicity agent.'

While Scannell (2014, p. 180) sees certain value in analysing media events as a form of exercise of power, which can mask social inequality in society and promote the existing hegemonic order (e.g., fascism aestheticizing politics), this criticism also stands as a deflationary view and does not do justice to Dayan and Katz's idea. Scannell (2014, p. 180) explains:

> [...] Ceremony and spectacle have always been part of public life in any society, and objections to them are as old as the events themselves. Puritanism has an iconoclastic dislike of conspicuous public display which offends its austere worldview. Utilitarianism grumbles that such things are a waste of time and money, both of which could be better spent on less idle and more practical things. By any cost-benefit analysis, ceremonial events are irrational. They are neither useful nor necessary. To be sure, issues of power and inequality are centrally important concerns in any society and any politics. But now and then, societies choose momentarily (as all of us do), to take time out from the grittiness of ordinary life and celebrate. Media events are precisely not to be judged by the usual political criteria and if they are, they will simply slip through your fingers like butter. Any political interpretation of media events is deflationary.

But even before Scannell's defence, Dayan and Katz both separately responded to some of the criticisms against their original theory and readjusted their ideas. In their article 'No More Peace! How Disaster, Terror and War Have Upstaged Media Events', Katz and Liebes (2007, 2010) suggest that the focus of analysis should indeed shift from conquests, contests and coronations to disaster, terror and war. According to Katz and Liebes (2007, p. 157):

> We believe that cynicism, disenchantment, and segregation are undermining attention to ceremonial events, while the mobility and ubiquity of television technology, together with the downgrading of scheduled programming, provide ready access to disruption. If ceremonial events may be characterized as 'co-productions' of broadcasters and establishments, then disruptive events may be characterized as 'co-productions' of broadcasters and anti-establishment agencies, i.e. the perpetrators of disruption.

Furthermore, Katz and Liebes suggest that marathons of terror, natural disaster and war — media disasters — should be distinguished from media events as a separate genre, as these mediatized disasters have become far removed from the ceremonial roots of original media events (Cottle, 2006a; Liebes, 1997; Liebes & Blondheim, 2005). In more recent work, scholars of media events (e.g., Sonnevend, 2016; Zelizer, 2018) argue that none of the earlier forms of media events have in fact disappeared, but they continue to exist side by side. Our argument is that this is one of the aspects of hybrid media events. These events may be both ceremonial and disruptive, and the emphasis may shift during the course of events, depending among other things on the context out of which these typically global events have unfolded.

To revert to the responses of the original authors, Daniel Dayan (2010), in his article 'Beyond Media Events: Disenchantment, Derailment, Disruption', also revised his thinking about media events. For him, the 'macabre accoutrements to televised ordeals, punishments, and tortures' and the emphasis on 'stigmatization and shaming' in today's mediatized public events have caused media events to lose their potential to reduce conflict; instead, they 'foster divides, and install and perpetuate schisms' (Dayan, 2010, pp. 26–27). As a result, media events, in Dayan's revisit to the theory, tend to lose their distinct character and instead gravitate towards other genres. New media events are no longer clearly differentiated entities, but are spread out on a continuum. Dayan (2010, p. 27) suggests that this 'banalization of the format' produces what he calls 'almost' media events. Dayan reminds us that the pragmatics of media events have changed as messages have become multiple, audiences selective and social networks ubiquitous. Dayan

(2010, p. 27) summarizes the difference between televised, ceremonial media events and media events of contemporary media circumstances:

> Interpersonal networks and diffusion processes are active before and after the event, mobilizing attention to the event and fostering intensive hermeneutic attempts to identify its meaning. But during the liminal moments we described in 1992, totality and simultaneity were unbound; organizers and broadcasters resonated together; competing channels merged into one; viewers gathered at the same time and in every place. All eyes were fixed on the ceremonial centre, through which each nuclear cell was connected to all the rest.

Dayan leaves his reader in a state of scepticism. For him, the most likely consequences in today's 'contested territory of media events' are disenchantment and the loss of the 'we' — the most critical functions of media events (see also Dayan, 2006). Viewed from the present perspective, however, the ideas of enchantment and 'we' have certainly not disappeared, even in today's violent media events of hybrid appeal. Rather, we argue, we have seen an intensification of 'we' as it continues to reach new audiences in the present digital media environment. We may call this yet another hybrid aspect of current violent media events with global appeal.

1.3. On the Hybridization of Media Events

Among the attempts to develop media event theory in the global, digital framework, beyond the national and TV broadcasting context, the work of Nick Couldry and Andreas Hepp has been particularly influential. Hepp and Couldry (2010, p. 9) argue that in theorizing about media events today, we should not perceive them as 'placed' at a defined locality, but rather as disembedded, or even ubiquitous communicative practices. That is, we should understand media events today as translocal, transcultural and transnational phenomena articulated by a connectivity of different actors, platforms and communication processes (see also Hepp, 2015; Latour, 2005). Understood in this way, media events may be structured at once around relatively centralized power structures, such as national and global mainstream media — say the BBC or CNN — and multicentric power structures such as social networking sites and the communication technologies embedded in those structures (cf. Hepp & Couldry, 2010, p. 9).

To follow Couldry's (2012, p. 79) insight in today's world, media events may have become rarer, yet the media's special relationship with events and the larger social world it addresses remains crucial. Research therefore needs to give greater emphasis to the processes of mediation and/or mediatization of events, instead of focusing on one medium only (such as TV). Couldry and Hepp's revised definition (in Couldry, 2012, p. 79) describes media events as:

> Certain thickened, centering performances of mediated communication that are focused on a specific thematic core, cross different media products and reach a wide and diverse multiplicity of audiences and participants.

This definition fits well the current condition in which the media is deeply involved in competition for attention and in an explicit battle for legitimacy (symbolic value) and survival (economic value) (see also Couldry, 2012, p. 79).

Julia Sonnevend's (2016) work on global iconic events provides yet another important perspective for the analysis of today's media events of global and digital appeal — that is, the significance of narratives and their circulation in today's media events. Sonnevend (2016, p. 2) has a special interest in what she calls global iconic events as 'news events that the international media cover extensively and remember ritually'. In her analysis, global iconic events have the capacity to transcend national boundaries in a lasting manner. However, Sonnevend claims (2016, p. 2) that global iconic events are never universal. This is to say that even though they can be transported from one context to another, they are not necessarily transported by everyone and to everywhere. Sonnevend (2016, pp. 2–3) explains: 'Global iconic events touch many hearts, but they do not have the same meaning for everyone. International news events enter a strongly fragmented political and journalistic space, which makes it hard for them to get unequivocal international recognition.' Global iconic events are thus always contested or ignored in some place.

Furthermore, Sonnevend is interested in global ceremonial events and in rethinking how narratives travel (across time, space and media platforms) in such events in the present global and digital context (Sonnevend, 2016, p. 20). She suggests that these events have five narrative dimensions: (1) foundation: the narrative prerequisites of events;

(2) mythologization: the development of their resonant message and elevated language; (3) condensation: the encapsulation of an event in a simple short narrative, and a recognizable visual scene; (4) counter-narration: stories that go against the prominent event narrative and (5) remediation: the ability of the event to travel across multiple media platforms and changing social and political contexts (Sonnevend, 2016, p. 3).

To sum up, then, the debate on media events is still very much alive, and new theoretical angles are being introduced into the discussion around those spectacular moments of history in which something exceptional and unique breaks the flow of ordinary and mundane life and calls for mediatized participation. Many scholars of media events agree today that while the media environment has changed radically since the late 1980s and early 1990s when Dayan and Katz wrote *Media Events*, the interest in making and shaping media events, whether ceremonial and/or disruptive in nature, remains undiminished. The phenomenon of media event still exists in social reality today and can be studied as a category that is reformed in the digital media.

Present-day research on media events gives more focus to the growing role of new global communication technology in enabling today's media events and to the complex relationships between the actors and media platforms involved in making and participating in those events on a global scale (Vaccari et al., 2015). These changing conditions also pose a major challenge for rethinking not only what today's media events are, but what they do in telling the story of 'us' (and often 'them') in these global high moments of ceremony and/or disruption. Therefore, Barbie Zelizer (2018), Julia Sonnevend (2016), Annabelle Sreberny (2016) and other scholars give special attention to the narrative elements and the contextual frameworks in which today's media events appear and are made sense of.

We argue in this book that to analyse today's media events as hybrid means to pay special focus to the complex interplay between the different actors, messages and platforms that contribute to the making of a media event. To be more specific, this hybrid interplay, we claim, is created in a complex network of mass media, internet-based and mobile communication technologies, and it creates relatively fluid social intensifications between and among different actors. As such, hybrid constellations in today's media events may comprise elements of ceremonial mass media communication, but they increasingly often converge with contemporary forms of vernacular mass self-communication (see also Castells, 2009).

Furthermore, we acknowledge that the level of connectivity in hybrid media events between 'official' and 'viral' narratives of the event may vary greatly from case to case. This means that the idea of the 'whole world' watching, as applied in the original media theory (Dayan & Katz, 1992), needs to be approached as an experience that is scattered onto a multiplicity of screens. As Julia Sonnevend (2016) reminds us, while people may be taking part in a hybrid media event on a global, iconic scale, they are connected to it in different ways. They will be using different communication media to follow the event, associating with different — and even conflicting — narratives circulating in connection with the event, and so feel connected with different groups and identities involved in the event. What follows as a consequence is a multiplicity of shared experiences around a hybrid media event and related sociality.

And yet, this ubiquity of a hybrid media event by no means diminishes its social and cultural power in the present world. Quite the contrary, we argue that today's hybrid media events may be perceived as more global, visible and omnipresent than ever; they speak to a larger and more heterogeneous audience than ever. Consequently, the question of power embedded in social integration as underlined in Dayan and Katz's (1992) original theory needs to be addressed at several levels. Multiple collective imaginations and related social, cultural and political implications may be simultaneously at play, and they may also be in conflict with each other. As we will argue later in this book, this condition of multiple narratives and related collective imaginations and the symbolic battles and uneven hierarchies between them may paradoxically heighten the significance of simplified and condensed narratives that have wide-ranging cultural, historical, political and religious resonance in communicating terror and violence in today's world.

1.4. The Five Elements of Hybrid Media Events

To further advance our understanding of hybridity in today's media events, we use five analytical elements. We have extracted these elements from our categorization of the key narrative components of the media event in focus (what happened in the *Charlie Hebdo* attacks) and their production (how and by whom were these happenings brought about) and with what consequences.

We call these elements the five As of global hybrid media events. The five As are as follows: actors, affordance, attention, affect and acceleration. In a nutshell, the first two elements — actors and affordances — form the environment of the hybrid media event. The third element — attention — is the motive power or fuel of the hybrid media event, and the fourth — affect — is the element that accumulates and directs attention and its circulation. Finally, the fifth A — acceleration — is a consequence of all other elements and of what takes place in a hybrid media event because of the conditions formed in the elements.

1.4.1. Actors

It is impossible to think about the past, present or future in media events without considering the actors who create those events (see, e.g., Wagner-Pacifici, 2017). In this book, we draw particularly on Latour's (2005) ideas about actors and agency and the idea of human and non-human connectivity in making and shaping today's media events. In line with Latour (2005, p. 5), we are specifically interested in those associations and connections between different types of actors (individual, non-human and collective) that appear in present media events and how the sense of the social and belonging is created in those human–non-human encounters.

Our present-day media events typically involve multiple actors. In addition to more traditional orchestrators of media events, such as journalists in mainstream news media, PR professionals, officials and the political establishment, we find that today, ordinary media users, different activist groups and perpetrators (in this case terrorists) are also actively involved in creating and maintaining media events. As discussed above, the social reality of events is brought to the fore through complex processes of computational logics and algorithmic constellations. Simply put, the more we click and share certain types of materials related to the event, the more we are offered those contents on our screens and in our news feeds. José van Dijck (2013) calls this quantified sociality. This requires a methodological orientation that enables scholars to empirically trace those human and technological associations and encounters in a variety of networks created in and around today's media events. So, while actors have always played a central role in creating media events, we argue that for a rigorous analysis of today's hybrid media events, it is necessary to broaden our category of actors and include non-human actors and agency in those events, and further-more to pay closer attention to the globalized and intensified dynamics between the different actors contributing to the event.

1.4.2.   Affordance

Today's media events are made possible in and by digital communica-tion technology. As discussed above, our understanding of the concept of actor takes into account both the human and the non-human actor and the individual and the non-individual actor, as well as their rela-tionship with the broader media environment and social structure. The concept of affordance provides the theoretical link between social orga-nizing in the media event (by different actors) and the technology avail-able for communicating it and bringing it into social existence in a certain way. The concept of affordance, then, allows research to reach beyond the division between actor and structure (Faraj & Azad, 2012).

The roots of the concept of affordance lie in the issue of the relation-ship between human perception and technology. Initially, James J. Gibson (1979, pp. 129–130) saw affordance in terms of what things enable us to do, as a concept that 'is neither an objective property nor a subjective property; or it is both if you like… It is equally a fact of envi-ronment [artefact] and a fact of behavior [action]. An affordance points both ways: to the environment and to the observer' (additions by Faraj & Azad, 2012, p. 249). This means that a same object affords dif-ferent possibilities of action depending on the conditions of the actor. Affordance is the reciprocal and immediate relationship between the environment and organism (Faraj & Azad, 2012, p. 249). In the case of a media event, the affordance of YouTube may be different to a perpe-trator who makes and shares a martyr video by using that communica-tion technology before an attack than it is for an ordinary media user who uses that same technology to make a mourning video to pay respects to the victims killed in the attack and shares it on YouTube.

Our aim in this book is to take a relational view on the concept of affordance and to see affordances as emergent properties of 'what can be done' (Stoffregen, 2003 in Faraj & Azad, 2012, p. 249). In our under-standing of the concept, affordances are thought of as opportunities for action rather than properties of the environment. An object in the environment offers different possibilities of action depending on the actor's motivation and abilities (Faraj & Azad, 2012, pp. 250–251). Importantly enough, these properties should be seen as not just personal, but also social properties. Questions of ethnicity, language and gender, and questions of power, social status and profession are social conditions that influence the possible affordances in using social media technologies.

1.4.3. Attention

Contemporary media events offer an unlimited supply of media contents, and it is in principle possible for anyone to engage in media production. Human attention, however, is necessarily limited in supply (Webster, 2014). This condition is described as the marketplace of attention (Webster, 2014) or attention economy (Davenport & Beck, 2001), highlighting the fact that attention is now the motive force of circulation in the contemporary media environment. In practice, the tracking of attention (in the form of clicks, likes, shares, etc.) has become the means with which internet platforms gain their revenue.

The growth of global internet advertising and social media platforms has profoundly affected the business logics and advertising markets of news media industries, which used to operate on a national basis. As a result, even journalistic media have been driven to search for clicks and shares. In other words, the actors with an interest in and capability for attention management in contemporary, hybrid media events are now many and varied: they are not just limited to the journalistic media institutions that before the internet used to set the agenda for public discussions. In a hybrid media event, anyone with a mobile phone or computer, internet access and Twitter account can circulate messages publicly. This, however, does not necessarily mean the message will gain wide attention. That depends on the power relationship between the actors involved and on their resources and abilities to use technological and social affordances. That said, the division of resources in present-day hybrid media events is highly unequal, and professional news institutions such as CNN are in the position to invest much greater resources in winning the battles of attention in those media events.

In the symbolic battles waged in today's media events, all actors — institutional, professional, terrorist and civil — are keen to manage attention. Depending on the situation, they may either vie for attention or try to avoid attention. Conscious communication strategies are intertwined with less intentional commentary and media texts that become key tools in creating and shaping global media events of terrorist violence. All this seeking of attention in today's media events affects public discussions. Attention is accumulated and directed through the circulation of memes, visuals, texts and videos. Also, affective contents tend to accumulate attention more easily than neutral contents (see also Papacharissi, 2015).

1.4.4. Affect

In this book, we have found Sara Ahmed's (2004a) understanding of affect particularly useful. Ahmed views affect and emotions as social and cultural practices rather than individual psychological states. She points out that affects are not properties of signs or commodities, but are produced in the circulation of signs or commodities. Affect, then, is a means to gain attention, accumulate attention and manage meanings. Ahmed's discussion of hate as affective economy is relevant to our analysis of the hybrid media event, as she points out that 'emotions do not positively inhabit anybody or anything, meaning that "the subject" is simply one nodal point in the economy, rather than its origin and destination' (Ahmed, 2004a, p. 46). In the circulation of hate, sticky, affective words and metonymic connections are particularly important. Connecting 'terrorism' with 'Islam' is one of these sticky connections that has continued to gain in strength since 9/11 (Ahmed, 2004b). Ahmed also points out that in discourses of 'war on terrorism', the issue of public mourning or grievable and ungrievable bodies becomes a question of legitimate and illegitimate lives (see also Butler, 2004). What is more, the process of sticky affects circulating and gathering attention (and sidelining attention from other matters) in today's hybrid media events is continuing to gather speed, spearing simultaneously into a multiplicity of digital media platforms. This intensified circulation of affects adds an important dimension to the analysis of today's hybrid media events, as it affects and shapes the construction of the social reality of those events.

1.4.5. Acceleration

As pointed out above, the element of speed has special relevance to the analysis of today's hybrid media events. The idea of speed points towards the temporal and spatial acceleration of media events. In this condition, information in the form of images, news, messages, memes and videos travel fluidly between actors, platforms and devices and cross geographical and cultural borders at ever-increasing pace. To follow

John Urry (2007), there is no stasis in present media events, only processes of creation and transformation. This idea draws our attention to the speed and de-stability of movement in today's hybrid media events. In his book *Empires of Speed: Time and Acceleration of Politics and Society*, Robert Hassan argues that the temporal speed of contemporary society reaches into every realm of the social, bringing rapidity to the very core of our collective and individual existence (2009, p. 8). The logic of 'social acceleration', which is forcing us to work faster, move faster and think faster, is also central to creating and maintaining today's media events. The social norms of digital media have it that people are expected to connect faster, share faster and participate constantly (see also van Dijck, 2013). Nevertheless, as Hassan (2009, p. 17) argues, '[t]he present Empire of Speed based upon computer-driven acceleration is one where there is no one in control because politics can no longer synchronize (keep up) with the pace of change that has become an end itself'. The same logic, we argue, prevails in hybrid media events of terrorist violence where perpetrators, authorities, journalists, victims, witnesses and other actors are able and expected to connect with each other faster than ever, with often unpredictable consequences.

The accelerated spatial and temporal movement of information in today's media events also enters into the conflicts, shaping them inside out and outside in. This has implications for their internal organization, external development as well as for their outcomes and consequences (cf. Cottle, 2014; Eskjær, Hjarvard, & Mortensen, 2015). The implications of acceleration are seen at all levels, from global (macro) to national (meso) and individual (micro), as the networked and digital 'world has become a singular, interconnected place where major changes tend to have effects and implications for nearly everyone' (Hassan, 2009, p. 7). Finally, to follow John Urry (2007, p. 6), we claim that issues of movement, of too little or too much, of the wrong sort or at the wrong time, are central to the workings and outcomes of present-day media events. This very much holds true in the case of hybrid media events of terrorist violence where the mediated movement of information may become a matter of life and death and a matter of media ethics in society.

1.5. Analysing Hybrid Media Events on Twitter and Beyond

For the scope of this book, Twitter offers a useful starting point for the study of hybrid media events. In this present 'event society' (Therborn, 2000, p. 42) or 'society of experience' (Huyssen, 2000, p. 25) saturated with media events, communication has also become an increasingly event-based activity (cf. Murthy, 2012, p. 1064). In this situation, Twitter has become a key platform for breaking news, and therefore events that draw attention tend to surface first on that platform. Also, Twitter provides rich data that shed light on other forms of media. Several media organizations, politicians and authorities use Twitter, and content and actors from other media platforms are also present through message circulation (cf. Kraidy & Mourad, 2010). As Dhiraj Murthy says: 'Organizing social life by events presents opportunities for everyday people and traditional media industries to tweet side-by-side' (Murthy, 2012, p. 1064). In this context, Twitter has been described as a prominent symbol of change in the media landscape:

> If we allow ourselves to paraphrase the CNN effect of the 1990s, this changeover in the media landscape could be called the Twitter effect. As was true for the CNN effect, which was caused by more than just the CNN organization, the Twitter effect must also be considered as a symbol of a much broader phenomenon, concerning several online tools oriented to the publication of user-generated, real-time content (Twitter, Facebook, YouTube, etc.). (Bruno, 2011, p. 8)

Previous studies on Twitter events (such as political elections or sport events) also give emphasis to the role of audiences in co-producing a media event, alongside traditional mass media (cf. Girginova, 2015; Kreiss, Meadows, & Remensperger, 2014). Furthermore, in the field of crisis communications, Twitter has been at the centre of many discussions. From the Arab Spring to the 2011 London riots, Twitter has been identified as a prominent platform for citizen communication in several revolutions, protests and movements, connecting people and bypassing gatekeepers, whether they be the authorities or journalists (cf. Bennett & Segerberg, 2012; Procter, Vis, & Voss, 2013). From the journalistic viewpoint of crisis reporting, the first ever 'Twitter disaster' was the 2010 Haiti earthquake: in the first 24 hours following the quake, news organizations depended for their coverage on social media, especially the easily accessible flow of information on Twitter (Bruno, 2011). In times of crisis, ordinary people can actively produce information, and they can also link and share published news stories from mainstream news media (Utz, Schultz, & Glocka, 2013).

In this book, too, Twitter provides an important empirical context for the analysis of hybrid media events. We gained access to Twitter data through a third-party social media analytics service called Pulsar (http://www.pulsarplatform.com/). The data were collected using three search and filtering criteria: search terms, time window and language. All the tweets collected were sent during 7–16 January 2015. The phrases and hashtags gathered included: 'je suis charlie', 'je ne suis pas charlie' or 'je suis ahmed' or any of the hashtags #jesuischarlie, #jenesuispascharlie or #jesuisahmed. Furthermore, all tweets selected were written either in English, French or Arabic. The total number of tweets was 5.2 million, of which 1.5 million were original tweets and the rest retweets.

While the Twitter data provide the starting point for our quantitative analysis and offers empirical evidence of the networked relationships between the different actors involved in the *Charlie Hebdo* attacks, we also use other media materials such as stories published by online news media and other social media in order to gain a clearer understanding of the workings of this hybrid media event. This complementary material consists of a wide range Anglo-American and French news media such as CNN, *The New York Times*, *The Guardian*, the *Daily Mail*, *Le Figaro*, *Le Monde* and *Libération* through to other international media houses such as *Al Jazeera English*. Finally, our analysis of the *Charlie Hebdo* attacks as a hybrid media event also made use of other social media platforms such as YouTube and Facebook.

1.5.1. Three Empirical Phases

The empirical analysis of today's hybrid media events requires a specific methodological setting. We call it a multi-method model, which sets the rhythm of the analysis and closely integrates quantitative and qualitative research approaches (for a more detailed description of our methodological approach, see Sumiala et al., 2016). More specifically, in this book we combine computational social science — automated content analysis (ACA) (Boumans & Trilling, 2016) and computational social network analytics (SNA) — with a qualitative approach, particularly digital ethnography. The different approaches follow a certain chronological order and are brought into dialogue as follows:

1. the first empirical outline of the event is provided by means of digital ethnography;
2. the digital field for research is constructed by means of automated content analysis and social network analytics; and

3. an in-depth interpretation of what (substance/content) is circulating and how this material connects with the 'where' in the hybrid media environment, creating the links and connections necessary for the social meaning making and interpretation of the event in a hybrid media environment, are provided by digital ethnography.

As explained above, global hybrid media events interrupt the daily routines of the media and people's everyday life. This moment of massive media saturation and circulation of information produces the first methodological challenge for the study of hybrid media events. This first phase of chaotic information flow requires a digital ethnographic perspective in which the events are followed and organized into a timeline. In the case of the *Charlie Hebdo* attacks, we started our pilot study while the events were still unfolding. As digital ethnographers, we traced the news in the mainstream media, such as the BBC, *The New York Times*, *The Guardian* and *Le Monde*, as well as on Twitter, YouTube and Facebook. Our personal media streams also included national news outlets, as well as friends and family members in our native Finland and around the world, reporting and commenting on the events from different local perspectives. We identified certain prominent messages, hashtags, posts, memes and images circulating in those media environments. To give one example, it was soon announced that the hashtag #JeSuisCharlie was the most-tweeted message in the history of Twitter, offering a simple and interesting lead to be followed in the course of events.

This first ethnographic phase of the analysis is best described as suggestive, and it may well be that its findings are challenged in the subsequent phases of quantitative and qualitative analysis. Yet it is a necessary stage for the process to follow, for it provides the first suggestive sketch of the initial chaotic information flow around the events. It offers crucial insight into the timeline of the event, into what might be interesting, relevant and peculiar about the incidents as they evolve, and so gives direction for the analysis in the next phase. As well as providing a timeline of the media event, this concrete stage of data gathering yields large volumes of field notes, screenshots, memes, images, videos and links.

In the next phase, social network analytics are applied to present a more general overview of communication around the events with more data. In the case of the *Charlie Hebdo* attacks, the media platform in focus was Twitter. In this so-called helicopter stage of the analysis, social network analytics are used to construct the research field and provide an overview of the data, and to map certain elements that are considered relevant based on the first phase of the pilot study. As explained above, the data collected prior to the analysis was acquired through the social media analytics platform Pulsar using several search words. We began with the hashtag #JeSuisCharlie and identified certain key groups: actors including ordinary media users and professional media houses. This helped us to empirically illustrate communicative networks created around the event — where and when they took place and how they existed in relation to each other.

In the third and final stage of the empirical analysis, the networks mapped by means of quantitative analysis and social network analytics and its visual illustrations are revisited from an ethnographic point of view. The quantitative analysis draws a map of the field and provides orientation for the ethnographic immersion. It helps to uncover aspects and elements in the event that call for more detailed analysis, and so contributes to producing a more holistic understanding of the ways in which the event is created and made sense of in the hybrid media environment studied.

The fieldwork phase in a hybrid media environment integrally involves a dense description of the observations made in the form of field notes and data documentation and recording by any means available, including screenshots and prints (cf. Sumiala & Tikka, 2013). In order to capture the research object in a highly complex and dynamic environment, it is useful to go back to the timeline and re-evaluate the first sketch of the events against the quantitative framework and then to make any necessary readjustments. In this phase, the researcher needs to reassess the relationship of the incident with the larger event and the key nodal points in this process. This can be done by searching for facts connected with the events and identifying certain key elements such as time, place and people by collecting other online media materials. This can be a challenging task in the hybrid media environment, for hybrid media events host and entice myriads of interpretations, misunderstandings, rumours and intentional misinformation.

After reidentifying the basic elements in the event, the researcher can begin to add layers of meanings to the event. This can be done in two overlapping ways: it is possible, first, to conduct ethnographic fieldwork by following paths and trails of links, streams and algorithmic suggestions offered by Twitter and other social media platforms, but it may also be useful, second, to conduct digital ethnography by simultaneously approaching the event from different directions, for instance by using search engines to run searches on different online media sites.

In these overlapping processes, the digital ethnographer will develop a more nuanced and in-depth understanding of the event and eventually be able to make interpretations of those more or less visible and hidden representations, discourses, actors and symbols and related communicative practices that contribute to creating and maintaining different types of social imaginaries of solidarities, belongings and exclusions embedded with the media event.

A multi-method approach to studying hybrid media events can thus be described as a prismatic methodological tool. It helps to shed light on different empirical layers, aspects and elements in the material. This requires a careful and ongoing reflection of the empirical process.

1.6.   Structure of the Book

This book is structured as follows. In Chapter 2, we begin our empirical analysis of the *Charlie Hebdo* attacks as a hybrid media event by (re) constructing its main narrative storyline. We focus on the first 10 days after the shootings, up to the publication of the *Charlie Hebdo* 'survival issue' and its immediate aftermath. As we demonstrate in the second chapter, these days constitute the main narrative storyline of the event. It includes the rupture (the attacks, manhunt and killing of the perpetrators), the height of the public response (demonstrations in January followed by public funerals) and the climax (the publication of a new issue of *Charlie Hebdo*). In this chapter, we draw on Julia Sonnevend's (2016, p. 3) ideas of the narrative construction of the event and its five key dimensions as discussed above: foundation, mythologization, condensation, counter-narration and remediation. Our analysis in Chapter 2 is mainly based on digital ethnographic fieldwork conducted on various media platforms in phases one and three.

Chapters 3 to 6 provide an empirical analysis of the interplay between the narrative and hybrid elements (e.g., the five As) in the *Charlie Hebdo* attacks. The cases are selected for analysis based on their meaning, prominence, visibility and relevance in making sense of the media event. In Chapter 3, we draw on quantitative analyses of the Twitter data and identify the most popular and retweeted actors and hashtags in the attacks. In addition, we show how affordances between actors and technologies contributed to imposing communication between certain actors and messages.

In Chapter 4, we turn our empirical gaze to the aspect of attention and to how attention directs the process of meaning making in the

Charlie Hebdo attacks. In this chapter, we examine the circulation of attention in the *Charlie Hebdo* attacks by analysing the death of police officer Ahmed Merabet and the related public and official responses to his tragic death on the street. The empirical analysis of Merabet's media death is based on digital ethnographic fieldwork in phases one and three.

In Chapter 5, we investigate the aspect of affect in the *Charlie Hebdo* attacks and look at how the circulation of emotions contributed to shape sense-making in this media event. In particular, we focus on the mediatized rituals of public solidarity created around the slogan and meme 'Je suis Charlie' and its counter-rituals. Special attention is given to the ways in which those mediatized rituals were performed on various media platforms by diverse actors and for different purposes. The empirical material of this chapter is based on a combination of digital ethnographic analyses of Twitter data and other online media materials.

In Chapter 6, we examine acceleration as the last key element in the *Charlie Hebdo* attacks. Our empirical analysis is based on digital ethnography conducted on the two hostage situations in the attacks. In this chapter, we illustrate how the intensified circulation of actors and messages shaped the meaning making of the event and impacted on the roles of the parties involved, that is, the perpetrators, news media, hostages and officials.

In the concluding chapter, we revert to the interplay between terror and media events in the present digital condition. We summarize the key features of hybridity in the *Charlie Hebdo* attacks and critically reflect upon the ethical consequences of this hybridization of today's media events and how they influence the present media research on globalized societies, using the *Charlie Hebdo* attacks as our case in point.

Chapter 2

Creating a Media Event

2.1. Many Beginnings

Peter Hervik and colleagues (2008, p. 29) say that for something to count as an 'event', it should have a recognizable beginning, climax and end. In what we call 'real life', events are certainly not as clear-cut as that. In the context of academic writing and media reporting, events are always the outcome of selection and rejection processes based on some implicit or explicit criteria. Some incidents and actors may be considered to be part of the event; others may be ignored and excluded from the main narrative.

In this chapter, we begin our empirical analysis of the *Charlie Hebdo* attacks as a media event by investigating how the main narrative of the event (and some threads in the counter-narratives) was constructed. We do this based on the coverage and representation of the incidents in online news media and social media. Rather than simply describing what the media reported and represented of what happened between 7 January 2015 and the publication of the new *Charlie Hebdo* issue on 14 January, we also wish to discuss some of the narrative preconditions for the event and how those preconditions may contribute to the interpretation and sense-making of the incidents. To this end, we draw on Julia Sonnevend's (2016) work and the idea that iconic global media events always include narrative prerequisites that provide a framework for interpreting them. These narrative prerequisites can be thought as mnemonic schemes — to use the words of Barbie Zelizer (2018) — that guide and direct the process of interpreting the incidents in and beyond the immediate media representation. Later in this chapter, we also apply Sonnevend's (2016) other criteria in analysing global media events, such as mythologization, condensing messages into slogans, the role of counter-narratives and the remediation of the event. But the first question we have to address concerns the beginning.

2.2.   *Charlie Hebdo* — A 'Bête et Méchant' Newspaper

Charlie Hebdo, a French satirical newspaper, was a highly controversial institution even before the attacks. It had a chequered history of bans, rebirths, disputes and lawsuits, as well as enjoying international recognition. One example is the PEN/Tony and James Coodale Freedom of Expression Courage Award that was given to *Charlie Hebdo* after the attacks,[1] a decision that drew criticism from several well-known writers (Yuhas, 29 April 2015).[2]

The *Charlie Hebdo* newspaper first appeared in 1970 to companion the magazine *Hara-Kiri*, which was established in 1960 by French humourists, authors and editors Georges 'Professeur Choron' Bernier and Francois Cavanna. In 1970, *Hara-Kiri* was banned for mocking the death of former French President Charles de Gaulle. In November 1970, de Gaulle died in his home village of Colombey-les-Deux-Églises, and the publication released a cover which ridiculed the popular press's coverage of de Gaulle's passing. The *Hara-Kiri* headline declared: 'Tragic Ball at Colombey, one dead'. This was a direct reference to a disastrous fire in the Club Cinq-Sept nightclub, where 146 people died.

Hara-Kiri was banned, but its cartoonists and journalists refused to be silenced. They skirted the ban by launching a new newspaper, *Charlie Hebdo*. The new name was derived from a comics magazine called *Charlie Mensuel*, that is, *Charlie Monthly*. Charlie, in turn, was said to have taken its name from Charlie Brown, the lead character of *Peanuts* created by Charles M. Schulz — as well as poking fun at the de Gaulle episode. The publication ceased in 1981, but was resurrected in 1992.

Charlie Hebdo's predecessor *Hara-Kiri* called itself 'bête et méchant' ('stupid and nasty'), setting the satirical tone for the publication's style and political exercise. Its pet topics have included (far) right-wing politics and politicians, as well as religion (namely Catholicism, Islam and Judaism). In terms of genre(s), *Charlie Hebdo* features cartoons, reports, polemical commentary and jokes. The publication describes itself as secular, political and jubilant:

---

[1]https://pen.org/2015-pen-goodale-freedom-expression-courage-award (Retrieved 17 August 2016).
[2]https://www.theguardian.com/books/2015/apr/29/writers-join-protest-charlie-hebdo-pen-award (Retrieved 6 September 2017).

Charlie Hebdo is a punch in the face...

Against those who try to stop us thinking.

Against those who fear imagination.

Against those who don't like us to laugh.

Charlie Hebdo is an angry magazine, a paper that takes the p**s.

It's a weekly with a wallop, a digest with a dream.

It's a periodical that argues and a journal that thinks.

It's a gazette of the grotesque — because that's what so much of life and politics is.

It's a rag that has nothing to lose in the afterlife for the laudably simple reason that there is no afterlife.

Charlie Hebdo has no need of God, nor any need of Wall Street. Charlie doesn't need two cars and three cellphones to be happy.

To be happy, *Charlie Hebdo* draws, writes, interviews, ponders and laughs at everything on this earth which is ridiculous, giggles at all that is absurd or preposterous in life. Which is to say — very nearly everything.

Because life is so awfully short that it would be a pity to spend it whining in dismay instead of laughing it up a storm.[3]

The newspaper's naughty laughter has also angered many people, long before the Kouachi attacks. *Charlie Hebdo* has been accused of being misogynist, racist and blasphemous. It has angered different religious groups, not only the French and global Muslim community. Protests against *Charlie Hebdo* have been voiced both in France and around the world.

In the post 9/11 world, one of the most prominent protests against *Charlie Hebdo* took place in 2006, after the newspaper had reprinted the Muhammad cartoons first published in the Danish newspaper *Jyllands-Posten*. The *Jyllands-Posten* controversy fuelled political commotion,

---

[3]https://charliehebdo.fr/en/ (Retrieved 17 August 2016).

demonstrations and boycotts in a number of Muslim countries. *Charlie Hebdo* commented on this controversy and published an image of a weeping Prophet Muhammad on its front cover. The prophet was lamenting that 'C'est dur d'être aimé par des cons' ('It is hard being loved by jerks'). The public reaction was vociferous (both for and against the newspaper), and *Charlie Hebdo* was sued by the Grand Mosque of Paris, the Muslim World League and the Union of French Islamic Organisations (UOIF), all accusing the newspaper of racism. Eventually, the French court found *Charlie Hebdo* not guilty.

Five years later in 2011, the *Charlie Hebdo* offices were firebombed with a Molotov cocktail, and the newspaper's website was hacked. The firebombing was a reaction to *Charlie Hebdo*'s front cover of 3 November 2011, in which it again featured a caricature of the Prophet Muhammad. Renamed 'Sharia Hebdo', the edition of the newspaper promised '100 lashes of whip if you don't die laughing'. The Prophet Muhammad was listed as editor-in-chief. The Sharia Hebdo issue was intended as a reaction to the (re)introduction of Sharia law in certain Muslim countries. The newspaper said it wanted to comment on the oppression of women under Sharia and on cruelty against sexual minorities, including practices such as stoning, flogging and hand/foot/tongue amputations. In this journalistic setting, the Prophet Muhammad as the newspaper's 'guest editor' was portrayed as a character representing the voice of reason and sense of humour. The Sharia Hebdo issue prompted a huge public backlash among others in the global Muslim community.

Charlie Hebdo received threats and insults via Facebook and Twitter, and its offices were burned down. No one was killed, but managing editor Charb and some other prominent people on the newspaper staff were placed under police protection. In an act of solidarity, managing editor of the French newspaper *Libération*, Nicolas Demorand, made the newspaper's offices available to the *Charlie Hebdo* staff and dedicated a four-page supplement to their cartoons. The social media turmoil continued, and eventually the *Charlie Hebdo* website was hacked. Facebook reacted to the negative publicity surrounding *Charlie Hebdo* and temporarily suspended it.

In 2012, *Charlie Hebdo* once again published images of the Prophet Muhammad, some of which portrayed the Prophet in the nude. The publication of these images coincided with international controversy surrounding a YouTube film made by an American-based social media user. The film, called *Innocence of Islam*, was considered anti-Islam and blasphemous towards the Prophet Muhammad. It prompted loud protests and attacks against Western embassies in several Muslim countries.

The French political elites also stepped up their criticisms against *Charlie Hebdo*. Foreign Minister Laurent Fabius accused *Charlie Hebdo* of unnecessary provocation in a complex global political situation. Police protection around the *Charlie Hebdo* offices was increased. The newspaper refused to buckle, but continued its work and to defend its position in society.

Over the years, many French politicians and public intellectuals in France and Europe have commented on *Charlie Hebdo* and its style of commenting on politics and religion. Reactions have been divided both in France and elsewhere around the Western world. Some have accused *Charlie Hebdo* of inflaming passions and provoking violence, others have praised the newspaper for its defence of freedom for expression. Those expressing solidarity have also warned about the risks of self-censorship. Whatever the take on *Charlie Hebdo*, public interest in and around the newspaper has increased in the wake of these controversies, and new sales records have been set time and again. The cartoonists themselves have kept their noses to the grindstone. When one door has been closed, they have always found a new one to open, whether that has meant re-naming the publication, finding new offices or starting a new website or blog. The newspaper is still at work commenting on the world, politics and religion every week, in its 'bête et méchant' manner.

Although we may never come to fully know or understand the inner motivations of the Kouachi brothers, why and what they had in mind when they opened fire on the cartoonists and other people in the *Charlie Hebdo* offices, it is clear from the history of the newspaper that it had for a long time insulted the Muslim world and its respect and reverence of the Prophet Muhammad. This enmity between *Charlie Hebdo* and Muslims was only highlighted as the perpetrators shouted 'Allahu Akbar' ('God Is Great') and 'We have avenged the prophet' when they were leaving the building.

In this sense, the events at the *Charlie Hebdo* offices have many parallels in earlier confrontations between the news media and Muslims that stem from the publication of similar cartoons. The first that comes to mind is the case mentioned earlier where *Jyllands-Posten* in Denmark published a caricature of Muhammad in 2005, which led to violent protests and boycotts of Danish dairy produce in some Muslim countries. The violent reaction prompted heated debate in Danish and international news media. Many in the field of journalism took a sharply critical view of the Muslim protests and defended freedom of speech as a non-negotiable principle in Western societies. The political fallout of the event included increased polarization in Denmark and many other

Western countries, and an escalation of Islamophobia and right-wing nationalist populist movements (see, e.g., Eide, Kunelius, & Phillips, 2008; Hervik, 2018). The fact that *Charlie Hebdo* also contributed to this controversy by publishing its cartoons only underlines the connection between these two events.

But we could go back even further. Once the names of the *Charlie Hebdo* perpetrators, Saïd and Chérif Kouachi, were published, the news media began to dig up stories about the killers, their backgrounds and motivations. They found that the killers had grown up in poor suburban Paris, in the margins of French society. They were described as 'ghetto Muslims'. According to the papers, they had become radicalized jihadists because they wanted to belong and to have an identity (*The Guardian*, 12 January 2015).[4] *The Guardian* reported that Chérif Kouachi had been arrested and imprisoned in 2005 when he was travelling to Syria and Iraq in order to fight against the USA. The paper described Chérif Kouachi's life as follows:

> Chérif Kouachi was born in 1980 in Paris's diverse 10th arrondissement, which stretches from the Place de la République to the Gare du Nord. He was one of five children of Algerian immigrant parents. A source who knew Chérif Kouachi at the time of his first arrest on his way to catch the flight to Damascus in 2005 told the Guardian: 'He was abandoned very young; it's not clear if his parents couldn't look after the children or if his parents died. But he was put in care homes early — before the age of 10.' The care homes were far from Paris and his childhood was described as chaotic. When he reached 18 he returned to the North-East of Paris with his elder brother. He had a sports education qualification, but a poor school record and no other family support. When he became involved in the Buttes-Chaumont group[5] of friends he was back in Paris but living precariously.
>
> He was living almost like a homeless person, staying with someone but it was more of a mattress on the floor than a

---

[4]https://www.theguardian.com/world/2015/jan/12/-sp-charlie-hebdo-attackers-kids-france-radicalised-paris (Retrieved 10 August 2017).
[5]Jihadist group in Paris.

real home. He was very clearly marginalised. He was immature, just out of adolescence. He wasn't vindictive […] He went to the mosque, but went clubbing, made rap music, smoked hash, drank. He wasn't a hermit, the source said. (*The Guardian*, 12 January 2015)[6]

The news report on the past of the Kouachi brothers conveys a story of radicalization connected to the war in Iraq: Chérif Kouachi wanted to become a fighter in Syria and Iraq, but was arrested en route and imprisoned in France. One symbolic momentum in the brothers' radicalization stemmed from the Abu Ghraib prison scandal in Iraq, the torture and humiliation of Muslim prisoners by US soldiers. Photographs were leaked to the international media, causing great resentment and anger in the global Muslim community. *The Guardian* (Burke, 8 January 2015; Penketh, 8 January 2015)[7] reported that the atrocities at Abu Ghraib had angered the brothers and cemented their resolve to become terrorists.

These analyses are supported by more recent research on the *Charlie Hebdo* perpetrators among others by Olivier Roy (2016, pp. 19–39). The killers had a history of broken homes, petty crime, and they had become radicalized with their peers, rather than being influenced by the local mosque. Their knowledge of Islam was poor, yet (or perhaps for that reason) they were fascinated by radical jihadist propaganda. Finally, they were highly immersed in many elements of Western youth culture (e.g., drinking, gaming, rap music and sex).

These two brief examples suffice to illustrate the many potential beginnings for the *Charlie Hebdo* attacks discussed in the news media. While the shootings on 7 January launched the *Charlie Hebdo* attacks as a news event, much had happened before, and at the time of the shootings these pre-histories provided interpretive schemes with which to make sense of the incidents in the news media and the social media.

2.3. Remediation in Digital Media — Shootings Go Viral

As a news event, the *Charlie Hebdo* attacks began at 11:30 on the morning of 7 January 2015. On that Wednesday, French-Algerian brothers

---

[6]https://www.theguardian.com/world/2015/jan/12/-sp-charlie-hebdo-attackers-kids-france-radicalised-paris (Retrieved 10 August 2017).
[7]https://www.theguardian.com/world/2015/jan/08/paris-attack-suspect-cherif-kouchi-jailed-terror-offences-2008-charlie-hebdo (Retrieved 15 September 2017).

Saïd and Chérif Kouachi attacked the headquarters of the satirical newspaper *Charlie Hebdo*, killing 12 people. It was reported in the news that among the staff killed were cartoonists and journalists Stéphane Charbonnier (pen name Charb), director of publication since 2009; Jean Cabut (Cabu); Philippe Honoré (Honoré); Bernard Verlhac (Tignous); and Georges Wolinski (Wolinski).

In addition, the perpetrators killed economist and journalist Bernard Maris; columnist, psychoanalyst and psychiatrist Elsa Cayat (the only female victim who, like Wolinski, was of Jewish background, an ethnic dimension that will be relevant to the subsequent interpretation of the events), a visitor at the office; copy editor Mustapha Ourrad; Michel Renaud, a visitor at the office; maintenance worker Frédéric Boisseau; and police officer Franck Brinsolaro, who was bodyguarding Charb. After their attack, the Kouachi brothers returned to their car.

Following the onset of the news event, the next key incident in the chain of occurrences was the shooting of police officer Ahmed Merabet on the street. Merabet was patrolling the street when the Kouachi brothers fled the building. They shot Merabet and sped away in their getaway car. The reason this incident became so important in the course of events was its live coverage in digital media. An ordinary media user, Jordi Mir, happened to film the scene when the perpetrators were making their escape and shot the police officer. He posted the video on Facebook. The video went viral immediately, both in professional mainstream media and social media. Mir became famous for his video, but said in subsequent interviews that he had immediately regretted posting it on Facebook and had quickly removed it. By that time, however, the video had already been picked up by a large number of media houses and ordinary media users. *The New York Times* and many other media houses decided to publish the video. The next day, the image of Merabet's dead body on the street was splashed across the front pages of many international newspapers.

This incident provided graphic visual evidence of the attacks and contributed to shape the media and public response. The international news media quickly went into what Liebes and Blondheim (2005) call 'disaster mode' as they followed the manhunt in Paris. Newsrooms all over the world reported on the massive security operation that was developing as the Kouachi brothers managed to hijack another car and flee north out of Paris. News about the attack and the escape spread quickly from one media platform to another. The exhaustive remediation of the news only intensified its significance as a media event.

2.4. Mythologization of the Victims

2.4.1. *News Coverage and Global Mourning*

The next element of importance in the construction of the *Charlie Hebdo* attacks as a media event was the massive public reaction and response. It was not only that the global audience followed the unfolding incidents through the news media and on their screens, but many wanted to participate and comment on the attacks in the social media as well. One of the key instigators of the global wave of solidarity that followed in the wake of the *Charlie Hebdo* attacks was French journalist and artist Joachim Roncin. He first tweeted an image with the caption 'Je suis Charlie' for *Stylist Magazine* less than 20 minutes after the attack. The words 'Je suis Charlie' were printed in bold white letters against a black background. According to BBC News (Devichand, 3 January 2016),[8] this image was used 1.5 million times on the day of its publication and some six million times during the next week on Twitter, Instagram and Facebook. Additionally, the hashtag #JeSuisCharlie became the most tweeted message in the history of Twitter (Sumiala et al., 2016). The meme and related hashtag travelled quickly from one digital platform to another, and both were used by countless media users, both professional and non-professional, for diverse purposes. As is typical of the logic of the attention economy in a media event, the creator of the meme became an internationally recognized public figure and a topic of global news (see Potet, 9 January 2015).[9] In an interview with the BBC (3 January 2016), Roncin demonstrates a desire to give meaning to the public response to the events. He comments on his feelings and motivations in creating the meme and putting it in global circulation:

> 'I was deeply shocked, but I wasn't frightened.' [...] The slogan took off because 'we're trying to feel a community', he says. 'It is very reassuring to be all together whenever there is something horrible happening.' [...] for [...] Joachim Roncin, the meaning of his slogan is still straightforward. 'Je suis Charlie' is just an expression of solidarity, of peace,' he says. 'And that's all.'

[8]http://www.bbc.com/news/blogs-trending-35108339 (Retrieved 15 September 2017).
[9]http://www.lemonde.fr/m-actu/article/2015/01/09/je-suis-charlie-c-est-lui_4552523_4497186.html (Retrieved 15 September 2017).

On the evening of 7 January 2015, many seemed to share Roncin's emotional response and attitude towards the attacks. Tens of thousands of people took to the streets not only in Paris and France, but across Europe and the world to show solidarity with those killed by the gunmen. In this public ritualized mourning and commemoration, the cartoonists were put at the centre of attention, as the slogan 'Je suis Charlie' suggests. In many messages associated with the slogan, the cartoonists were given a symbolic role as advocates not only of the French values of 'liberté, égalité, fraternité', but also the values of modern Western civilization. In line with Sonnevend's (2016) thinking, we argue that the mythical message of the event was crystallized and condensed around the hashtag and slogan 'Je suis Charlie' and its countless versions.

However, these kinds of symbolic identifications are often contested and challenged in the global media environment in different types of counter-narratives (see also Sonnevend, 2016). In some comments and messages in the digital media, the cartoonists were blamed for their views and actions, which their opponents considered blasphemous, misogynist and racist. Instead of bringing the fate of the cartoonists close to the mourners, these messages communicated a certain distance between the cartoonists as victims and the people participating in commemorating their death. The critics thought the cartoonists were responsible for fuelling conflicts between ethnic and religious groups in society and were therefore not worthy of public mourning. In this narrative, the 'true' victims were the ordinary Muslim people who were opposed to violence, but who had to suffer from the actions of both the cartoonists and the killers (cf. Todd, 2015).

The death of police officer Ahmed Merabet can also be interpreted to symbolize one important storyline in this counter-narrative. In the digital media, the slogan 'Je suis Ahmed' began to circulate alongside 'Je suis Charlie' and other versions, although in much smaller numbers. Figure 2.1 illustrates the use of the three hashtags on Twitter, that is #JeSuisCharlie, #JeSuisAhmed and #JeNeSuisPasCharlie ('I am not Charlie') in the first 10 days after the attacks.

Figure 2.1 clearly demonstrates the prominence of the 'Je suis Charlie' message, which can be considered to express identification with the satirical newspaper and its victims. And yet, at the same time as these condensed messages were travelling from one media platform to another, ritual communication in the form of performances of public solidarity as well as expressions of anger and frustration became hybridized in the event. Ritual performances of solidarity with the victims in

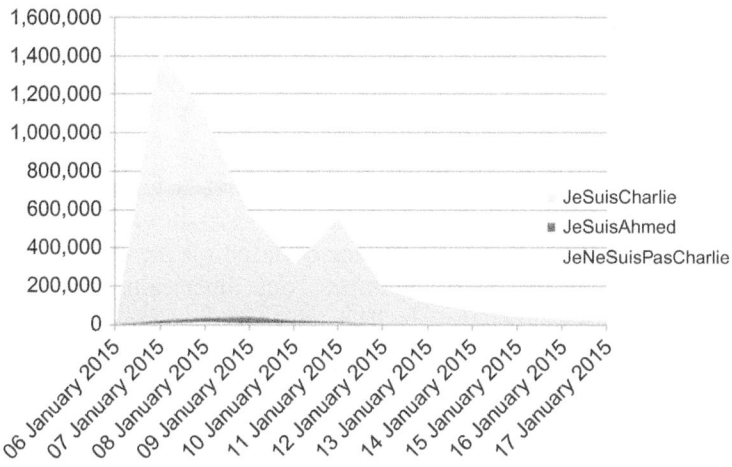

Figure 2.1: Number of Hashtags #JeSuisCharlie, #JeNeSuisPasCharlie and #JeSuisAhmed on Twitter during the First 10 Days after the Attacks.

the media typically involve sharing highly formatted messages of condolence that often include symbols of grief such as candles, flowers and notes. These messages and images can make reference to certain sites of high symbolic value, such as the crime scene, which may become spontaneous shrines and places of pilgrimage, or the symbolic heart of the city where the violence has taken place. In other cases, the posting and sharing of messages of solidarity can contain 'purely' virtual elements, such as in YouTube videos with such titles Rest in Peace (RIP) or Paying Tribute. This multiplication of the number of ceremonial participants who can take part in the event also brings about a polyphony of interpretations regarding what is occurring and what it signifies. Not all voices have similar power, but the potential for contradictory interpretations of this ritual act of granting the deceased a new identity also makes the rite unpredictable and difficult to control.

Furthermore, the ritual practices of posting messages and sharing symbols and images to show solidarity or express frustration followed a very similar pattern as in many other violent and terrorist incidents. There have been similar responses following school shootings in Finland, Germany and the USA, for instance (cf. Sumiala & Tikka, 2011). Other examples include the 9/11 terror attacks in the USA in 2001, the Madrid train bombings in 2004, the London bombings in 2005 and the Norway attacks in Oslo and Utøya in 2011.

The most ritualized and condensed message in the 'Je suis Charlie' event was not created out of thin air. The phrase 'I am' has a long history of expressing solidarity and support. One of the most famous versions appeared in the speech of President John F. Kennedy in June 1963, when he wanted to convey the US support for West Berlin during the Cold War by saying 'Ich bin ein Berliner' ('I am a Berliner'). Another well-known version of the slogan was published after 9/11 when the French newspaper *Le Monde* declared on the front page of its 12 September edition, 'Nous sommes tous américains' ('We are all Americans'). Ten years later in 2011, the Occupy Movement against social and economic inequality adapted the slogan into the form 'We are the 99%', in reference to the statistic that the wealthiest 1% of people own most of the world's riches. It was an expression of solidarity towards the 'rest' of the people who were paying for the mistakes made by the wealthiest 1% in the financial crisis.

In short, all of these ritualized practices of participating in the event and making and shaping the event on various media platforms also determined the tone of the attention given to the event and influenced the type of emotions that were attached to it.

2.4.2. The Manhunt Continues

The next day, on Thursday 8 January, the attackers remained at large and thousands of security personnel were deployed to comb an area some 90 kilometres from Paris where the two men had last been seen. Meanwhile, in Paris, reports were emerging that a policewoman had been shot dead, although links with the *Charlie Hebdo* attacks were not immediately confirmed. On Friday 9 January, police located the attackers in the Dammartin-en-Goële area. The brothers were chased to an industrial complex 35 kilometres from Paris where they seized a printing works and took a hostage. In east Paris, at around 12:30 p.m., a third gunman, Amedy Coulibaly, seized a Jewish supermarket, killed four people, and took hostages. It emerged that Coulibaly was responsible for killing Paris policewoman Clarissa Jean-Philippe the day before. Calling the French TV station BFMTV, Coulibaly said his attack was synchronized with the attacks of the Kouachi brothers and that they belonged to the same group of terrorists. He also threatened to kill his hostages unless the Kouachi brothers were allowed to walk free.

These simultaneous hostage situations again prompted intensive remediation of information where the perpetrators, authorities, hostages, journalists and ordinary people communicated via different channels at ever-increasing pace. After several hours of hostage standoff, police special forces stormed the market and killed Coulibaly. The Kouachi brothers were also killed by special forces on the same day.

2.4.3.   *Who Counts as a Victim?*

Questions such as who counts as a victim have special significance in narratives of violent media events. Not all individuals killed in terror attacks receive the same amount of public attention. As mentioned earlier, the *Charlie Hebdo* cartoonists were given the most attention in the global media as the victims of the attack. Their stories were shared with different publics and on different media platforms. The one surviving cartoonist Renald Luzier, pen name Luz, was interviewed and asked to speak on behalf of his dead colleagues. Luzier was also the cartoonist who drew the 'Je suis Charlie' Muhammad who appeared on the front cover of the survival issue.

The role of the victims at the kosher supermarket was much more ambivalent. Indeed, it was initially unclear whether the siege at the supermarket was part of the *Charlie Hebdo* attacks or a separate violent act. The news media reported that Coulibaly had shot dead policewoman Clarissa Jean-Philippe on Thursday 8 January, and on the next day, Friday 9 January, he had killed four customers after taking 15–19 hostages (depending on the source quoted) at a supermarket in Porte de Vincennes, south-eastern Paris. The media soon reported that Coulibaly probably had the assistance of his partner, a woman called Hayat Boumeddiene. The hostage standoff lasted some five hours, during which customers, including small children, had to go into hiding in the supermarket's cold storage room. Couliabaly's victims were: Yohan Cohen, 20, who worked at the kosher supermarket; Philippe Braham, 45, business manager at an IT company; Yoav Hattab, 21, student; and François-Michel Saada, 64, former pension fund manager (BBC News, 13 October 2016).[10] Before the police shot Coulibaly, he had made clear that his actions were connected to the *Charlie Hebdo* attacks, hence attempting to couple these two shootings into one narrative. The supermarket hostage situation was closely followed by national and international news media. Images were widely circulated in news media and on

---

[10]http://www.bbc.com/news/world-europe-34514244 (Retrieved 19 July 2016).

social networking sites. The local hero was Lassana Bathily, a young Muslim shop attendant who shepherded horrified customers to safety out of the freezer at the back of the supermarket.

Later, in April 2015, one new layer was added to the narrative as the six survivors of the hostage crisis decided to sue the French 24-hour news outlet BFMTV for its live broadcasts that — according to the survivors — had put their lives at risk by revealing, in a real-time broadcast, where they had been hiding (Sabin, 3 April 2015).[11] In 2016, they dropped their charges after reaching an out-of-court settlement with BFMTV (*Le Monde*, 8 January 2016).[12]

In the public mourning of the Jewish victims, slogans and placards declaring 'Je suis Juif' and #JeSuisJuif, in numerous different versions, began to circulate in the media among other signs and symbols of public grief. A key moment in this mourning was the public funeral in Israel. Four of the victims were flown to Israel and buried in Jerusalem. The funeral was attended by Israeli Prime Minister Benjamin Netanyahu. News clips from the funeral showed a deeply distraught, angry and mourning public (Line, 13 January 2015).[13] Witnesses interviewed at the funeral described the victims first and foremost as victims of antisemitism, something that they felt was on the increase in France and Europe at large. In short, the ritual attention given in the public mourning of the four Jewish victims (including Israeli flags, the Star of David and kippot) was heavily focused around the ethnic identity of the victims as Jews, a persecuted minority with a tragic history in Europe. In this connection it has to be acknowledged that two of the victims at the *Charlie Hebdo* offices also had a Jewish background: Elsa Cayat and Georges Wolinski. In these two cases, however, the element of ethnic identity was clearly played down in the victimhood narratives. Instead, the focus was firmly fixed on values associated with the victims' professional careers as part of the *Charlie Hebdo* story.

---

[11]http://www.independent.co.uk/news/world/europe/french-tv-channel-bfm-sued-over-coverage-of-paris-kosher-supermarket-massacre-that-allegedly-put-10154185.html (Retrieved 17 August 2016).

[12]http://www.lemonde.fr/police-justice/article/2016/01/08/hyper-cacher-les-otages-de-la-chambre-froide-retirent-leur-plainte-contre-bfm-tv_4844031_1653578.html (Retrieved 6 September 2017).

[13]http://www.telegraph.co.uk/news/worldnews/middleeast/israel/11342184/Jewish-victims-of-Paris-shootings-mourned-at-Israeli-funeral.html (Retrieved 17 August 2016).

Among the police officers killed, Ahmed Merabet was given more exposure than Clarissa Jean-Philippe and Franck Brinsolaro. This, we argue, had to do with the massive remediation of his killing. In other words, the visual evidence of Merabet's death contributed to shaping the narrative around the attacks and the differential emphasis given to their victims.

2.5. Condensation of Meaning(s)

2.5.1. The World Political Elites Demonstrate Solidarity

Yet another key moment in the narrative storyline of the *Charlie Hebdo* attacks was the world leaders' political response to the terror assaults. The then French President François Hollande, obviously, had a significant part in articulating the institutional response to the attacks. On 7 January 2015, Hollande gave the following speech to his countrymen at the Élysée Palace:

> My dear compatriots,
>
> [...] Today it is the Republic as a whole that has been attacked. The Republic equals freedom of expression; the Republic equals culture, creation, it equals pluralism and democracy. That is what the assassins were targeting. It equals the ideal of justice and peace that France promotes everywhere on the international stage, and the message of peace and tolerance that we defend — as do our soldiers — in the fight against terrorism and fundamentalism.
>
> France has received messages of solidarity and fraternity from countries around the globe, and we must take their full measure. Our response must be commensurate with the crime committed against us, first by seeking the perpetrators of this act of infamy, and then by making sure they are arrested, tried and punished very severely. And everything will be done to apprehend them. The investigation is now moving forward under the authority of the Ministry of Justice.
>
> We must also protect all public spaces. The government has implemented what is known as the Vigipirate Plan on

'attack' level, which means that security forces will be deployed wherever there is the hint of a threat.

Finally, we ourselves must be mindful of the fact that our best weapon is our unity: the unity of all our fellow citizens in this difficult moment. Nothing can divide us, nothing must pit us against one another, nothing must separate us. Tomorrow I will convene the Presidents of both assemblies as well as the political forces represented in Parliament to demonstrate our common resolve.

France is great when she is capable of rising to the test, rising to a level that has always enabled her to overcome hardships. Freedom will always be stronger than barbarity. France has always vanquished her enemies when she has stood united and remained true to her values. That is what I ask you to do: to join together, all of you, in every way possible; that must be our response. Let us join together at this difficult moment, and we shall win, because we are fully capable of believing in our destiny, and nothing can weaken our resolve.

Let us join together.

Vive la République et vive la France! (France Diplomatique, 7 January 2015)[14]

In this patriotic public address, Hollande framed the attacks as violent confrontations against the value of freedom and unity of France and urged the nation to join in to defend these values at the heart of the French republic. Many world political leaders joined Hollande and expressed their support. The British newspaper *The Independent* set the tone with an article titled 'World Leaders Unite in Condemning "Barbaric" Paris Killings' (Morris, 7 January 2015).[15] In addition to David Cameron (the then British Prime Minister), Queen Elizabeth II, the Pope, German Chancellor Angela Merkel and the then US President Barak Obama all publicly expressed their support. President Obama tweeted, 'Our thoughts and prayers are with the victims of this

---

[14]http://www.diplomatie.gouv.fr/en/the-ministry-and-its-network/events/article/attack-against-charlie-hebdo (Retrieved 10 August 2017).
[15]http://www.independent.co.uk/news/world/europe/charlie-hebdo-attack-world-leaders-condemn-barbaric-killings-9963622.html (Retrieved 11 August 2017).

terrorist attack and the people of France' (7 January 2015 on Twitter). The Pope condemned the attacks by saying, 'One cannot offend, make war, kill in the name of one's religion, that is, in the name of God' (Dias, 15 January 2015).[16]

Russian President Vladimir Putin's spokesman had this to say through the state-run Russian news agency TASS: 'Due to the tragic events in Paris where many people were killed as a result of the terrorist act, President Putin expresses condolences to relatives and all residents of Paris and the French people' (Tchernookova, 16 January 2015).[17]

The outpour of global support reached its climax in public demonstrations held on Sunday 11 January, in defence of the values of liberty and freedom of expression. Some 40 world leaders, including German Chancellor Angela Merkel, British Prime Minister David Cameron, Israeli Prime Minister Benjamin Netanyahu, President of the Palestinian National Authority Mahmud Abbas and French President François Hollande joined millions of people marching the streets of Paris (called 'marche républicaine', 'republican march') and elsewhere in France.

This public spectacle, performed by world leaders and ordinary people, made massive headlines in local, national and global news and created a storm of activity on social networking sites. Apart from messages of support and solidarity, it also generated considerable controversy and debate as to the motives of the world leaders who took part: who attended and who did not, why were they there, for what foreign or domestic political purposes?

2.5.2. Counter-narratives Challenge the Main Storyline

The world news media also reported on the countermarches and demonstrations against *Charlie Hebdo* and its supporters. *The Telegraph* (Parfitt, 19 January 2015)[18] reported on a Chechnya mass rally: 'Hundreds of thousands protest in Grozny as leader of Muslim republic accuses "morally degraded" West of organizing *Charlie Hebdo* attack in Paris.' The leader of Chechnya, Ramzan Kadyrov was reported as saying, 'We

---

[16]http://time.com/3668875/pope-francis-charlie-hebdo/ (Retrieved 5 September 2017).
[17]https://news.vice.com/article/russias-reaction-to-the-charlie-hebdo-attacks-and-what-it-says-about-putin (Retrieved 11 August 2017).
[18]http://www.telegraph.co.uk/news/worldnews/europe/russia/11355233/Chechnya-holds-mass-rally-against-Charlie-Hebdo-Prophet-Mohammed-cartoons.html (Retrieved 11 August 2017).

resolutely announce that we will never let anybody insult the name of the Prophet without punishment.'

These politicized public articulations of support and condemnation, on the one hand, and resistance and opposition, on the other, reflect the high tensions that were triggered by the *Charlie Hebdo* shootings, and their underlying political ideological, religious and cultural backgrounds. The politically motivated responses of the world political elite can be seen as manifestations of certain historical alliances between European countries (although twentieth-century history casts Germany's role in a rather problematic light), and between (Western) Europe and the USA. The Pope's public expression of solidarity can be explained in part not only by his symbolic role as a religious leader, but also by France's Catholic history — although the Catholic Church's role in the country has been regarded as highly problematic since the French Revolution and it has faced intense opposition from the political left. What is more, one of the most vociferous protagonists of this criticism and opposition has been none other than the *Charlie Hebdo* newspaper, which has published numerous cartoons ridiculing the Catholic Church and thus offended its supporters in France and elsewhere in the Catholic world.

The public articulations of solidarity and protest can also be considered from the point of view of how they treated Islam and its supporters. That is, the voices of solidarity (for the victims of the *Charlie Hebdo* attacks) provided an opportunity not only to support the republican values of liberty, equality and fraternity associated with *Charlie Hebdo*, but also to resist and take a stance against something (see also Titley, 2017). More often than not, this something was Islam and its supporters — both highly heterogeneous categories, but conveniently simplified for purposes of public demonstration. In these public reactions, Islam was more or less explicitly associated with terrorism, and its supporters regarded as (at least potential) terrorists. For those millions of people in the Muslim world who were protesting against *Charlie Hebdo* and its supporters, the expression of solidarity for the victims was tantamount to an expression of Islamophobia and a licence to continue with the blasphemy.

On 10 January 2015, *Al Jazeera English* (Al-Arian, 10 January 2015) published an article[19] on its opinion page titled, '*Charlie Hebdo* and

---

[19]http://www.aljazeera.com/indepth/opinion/2015/01/charlie-hebdo-twilight-western–201511063740106115.html (Retrieved 15 September 2017).

Western Liberalism: Islam Has Been Unfairly Criticised and Ridiculed in the West for Centuries'. The author, Abdullah Al-Arian, condemns uncritical attempts to defend freedom of expression in the West, saying that these efforts are conducted in such a manner that only serves to underline the West's long history of racism against Muslims. He continues:

> French society — and indeed, the global reaction — has been united in its condemnation of the attack, and French authorities mobilised the full strength of the state's law enforcement agencies to track down the assailants, who were killed after a standoff with police on Friday. As with most incidents of violence involving Muslims, however, the ensuing public discussion has revolved largely around resolute vows to uphold a fundamental value of western civilisation — the freedom of expression — and degenerated into recriminations about Islam's purported assault on that very freedom. As a result, the natural expressions of grief and sympathy on behalf of the victims have taken on the added quality of high-minded liberal support for the content of the *Charlie Hebdo* cartoons, irrespective of the publication's history of racism towards Muslims and people of colour.

In this frame of thinking, all the expressions of support by the world political leaders also shaped the dynamics of the hegemonic battle between 'the West' and 'the rest', and between religious and ethnic majorities and minorities. The comments of Vladimir Putin, for instance, have to be understood in the context of the geopolitical situation in Russia and its satellite countries such as Chechnya. Accordingly, one key context for Barak Obama's expressions of support and solidarity was provided by the 9/11 attacks and the consequent war in Iraq.

Another issue addressed in the expressions of support by leading politicians of the world was antisemitism. Israeli Prime Minister Benjamin Netanyahu tweeted a message addressed to all French and European Jews, saying 'the state of Israel is your home' (Nianias, 12 January 2015).[20]

---

[20]http://www.independent.co.uk/news/people/israel-is-your-home-benjamin-netanyahu-tells-french-jews-after-charlie-hebdo-rally-9971954.html (Retrieved 11 August 2017).

The Palestinian resistance organization Hamas promptly reacted to Netanyahu's public response to the events. Hamas stated that it 'condemns the attack against *Charlie Hebdo* magazine and insists on the fact that differences of opinion and thought cannot justify murder' (Dearden, 12 January 2015).[21]

According to *The Independent* (Dearden, 12 January 2015), Hamas rejected Benjamin Netanyahu's comments in which he compared the slaughter to Hamas's firing of rockets, which Israel said prompted its 50-day assault on Gaza in July. 'Hamas condemns the desperate attempts by [...] Netanyahu to make a connection between our movement and the resistance of our people on the one hand and global terrorism on the other', the statement said.

The presence of both Netanyahu and Abbas in the front line of the march only served to heighten the conflict between Israel and Palestine. According to *Euronews* (Gayle, 13 January 2015),[22] Netanyahu was supposedly asked by French President François Hollande to stay away, and he was not extended an invitation. *Euronews* reported that Paris was concerned about public attention being drawn to the Israel–Palestine conflict, instead of the march against terrorism. Abbas was not invited either. However, news sources said that Netanyahu had invited himself, and the French consequently invited Abbas (Gayle, 13 January 2015). The left-wing Israeli newspaper *Haaretz* criticized Netanyahu's appearance in Paris as 'a PR disaster' (Schechter, 12 January 2015).[23]

Palestinian President Mahmud Abbas's decision to participate in the demonstration also drew heavy fire from the world news media. The centre-right international online news site *The Commentator* (11 January 2015)[24] said:

> Nothing shows the West's lack of seriousness about terrorism more than the shameful presence of Palestinian leader Mahmoud Abbas at the mass demo in Paris. If the *Charlie*

---

[21]http://www.independent.co.uk/news/world/europe/paris-attacks-hamas-condemns-charlie-hebdo-massacre-after-netanyahu-makes-comparison-to-gaza-rockets-9970096.html (Retrieved 11 August 2017).
[22]http://www.euronews.com/2015/01/13/charlie-hebdo-israeli-paper-deletes-women-from-paris-march-photo (Retrieved 13 August 2017).
[23]http://www.haaretz.com/israel-news/.premium-1.636737 (Retrieved 8 September 2017).
[24]http://www.thecommentator.com/article/5523/shame_of_palestinian_leader_at_charlie_hebdo_demo (Retrieved 13 August 2017).

Hebdo massacre had taken place in Israel, Abbas would have named a square after the killers.

In some news reports, President Abbas's presence was contrasted with the demonstrations in Palestine against the *Charlie Hebdo* attacks and the show of public solidarity for the cartoonists. Reuters (Baker & Heneghan, 12 January 2015)[25] sums up the political outcome of Netanyahu and Abbas's appearance in the Paris demonstrations as follows:

> While the images on Facebook and Twitter are likely to buoy Netanyahu domestically, despite some criticism of his gauche behavior, going to Paris served Abbas less well. He has been vilified on social media and in newspaper cartoons for going to the French capital rather than visiting Gaza, which he has not been to since before last summer's war with Israel.

2.5.3. 'Huge Show of Solidarity in Paris against Terrorism'

Not just world leaders but also ordinary people marched on Sunday 11 January to pay tribute to the victims of the *Charlie Hebdo* attacks. The marches were reportedly the largest in the history of modern France. More than 1.6 million people took to the streets in Paris, and an estimated 3.7 million people demonstrated throughout France. *The New York Times* (Alderman & Bilefsky, 11 January 2015)[26] described the 'huge show of solidarity' in Paris:

> Responding to terrorist strikes that killed 17 people in France and riveted worldwide attention, Jews, Muslims, Christians, atheists and people of all races, ages and political stripes swarmed central Paris beneath a bright blue sky, calling for peace and an end to violent extremism.

In the most prominent narrative frame in Western news media, the demonstrations were interpreted as a (trans)national performance of solidarity and unity created around the values of freedom and peace.

---

[25]http://www.reuters.com/article/us-france-shooting-netanyahu-idUSKBN0KL16P 20150112 (Retrieved 13 August 2017).
[26]https://www.nytimes.com/2015/01/12/world/europe/paris-march-against-terror-charlie-hebdo.html (Retrieved 13 August 2017).

Place de la République, 11 January. Image by Olivier Ortelpa, Creative Commons Flickr.

Following Sonnevend's (2016) insight, news coverage of the protests in areas such as Chechnya, Yemen, Pakistan and the West Coast of Palestine can be interpreted as a counter-narrative to the Western response. Paradoxically, then, while the main narrative underlined solidarity and unity, the view taken in the counter-narratives was that those ritual expressions around 'Je suis Charlie' rather endorsed Islamophobia and blasphemy. These two narratives clearly conflict each other and hence undermine the plausibility of the message of unity in the main narrative of the attacks.

Finally, the public drama surrounding the *Charlie Hebdo* attacks climaxed with the release of a new *Charlie Hebdo* issue. The cover featured an image of the Prophet Muhammad carrying a 'Je suis Charlie' placard, under the title 'Tout est pardonné' ('All Is forgiven'). It sold almost 8 million copies,[27] and its making and publication became a media event in itself. *The Guardian* (Vulliamy, 18 January 2015)[28] reported on the making of the survival issue under the headline, 'A Week Inside of *Charlie Hebdo*'.

---

[27]The regular circulation of *Charlie Hebdo* is around 60,000.
[28]https://www.theguardian.com/media/2015/jan/18/charlie-hebdo-we-cant-let-this-change-our-cartoons-nor-will-it (Retrieved 15 September 2017).

The remaining editors had been invited to work at the offices of the newspaper *Libération*. *The Guardian* (Vulliamy, 18 January 2015) wrote:

> The edition was prepared around a large oval-shaped table in the corner at the offices of *Libération* — where it had also been produced after a firebomb attack in 2011. And last Wednesday, a crowd of visitors and reporters hauled itself up several flights of stairs to the cafeteria above *Libé*'s editorial floor, to hear cartoonist Renald Luzie — pen-named Luz — flanked by editor-in-chief Gérard Biard and doctor-writer Patrick Pelloux launch edition No 1,178 of *Charlie Hebdo*. We applauded as Luz took his place, awkwardly.
>
> [...] *Charlie Hebdo* cartoonist Renald Luzier, aka Luz, explains the magazine's latest front cover. [...] 'Then there was just this idea of drawing Muhammad: "I am *Charlie*". And I looked at him. He was crying. And I wrote above: "All is forgiven." It was the front page. We had finally found that damned front page, and it was our front page. Not the front page the world wanted, but that we wanted to make. Not the front page the terrorists wanted, because there are no terrorists in it. Just a man crying, a guy crying — it's Muhammad. I'm sorry we drew him again, but the Muhammad we drew is, above all, just a guy crying.'

On 14 January 2014, the date of issue, the international media showed pictures of people queuing for their copies in Paris and around the world. The survival issue itself became a collector's item.

2.6. After the 'Je Suis Charlie' Momentum

Going back to Sonnevend's (2016) frame of analysis, the global media event that was *Charlie Hebdo* had not only many beginnings, but also many endings. Although the publication of the survival issue marked an immediate closure of the event, the public debate around and beyond the *Charlie Hebdo* attacks continued for a long time, and is still continuing. Each year the 7 January anniversary calls for commemoration and reflection of the events.

In the public debate that followed the attacks, many asked what exactly was meant by 'being Charlie' and who had the right to identify themselves in such terms. Editors, reporters and cartoonists at *Charlie Hebdo* and their close circles voiced a degree of scepticism about the massive wave of public solidarity. *The Guardian* (Vulliamy, 18 January 2015)[29] wrote:

> During preparations for edition 1,178,[30] the procession through Paris by a million and a half people — marching behind political leaders from Britain, Israel, Turkey, Russia and elsewhere — was a parade of power that unsettled many on the paper, and caused some to stay away. Zineb el-Rhazoui, a Franco-Moroccan feminist working at the paper had marched and found it 'surreal, because usually we're alone, despised — and now we're part of this huge expression by the people. On the other hand, it was very surprising to find who our new friends are!' Laurent Léger, reporter with *Charlie Hebdo*, did not march. 'It had all become too political,' he explained. 'I didn't want to be next to those politicians, or shake their hands.' In the cruel aftermath, there was reflection as well as grief and defiance among those in the brasserie; and not a little bewilderment in the face of global attention. And unease too: at rising tension in the ghettos and at the notion that — as a French diplomat put it: 'Despite itself, *Charlie* is now a global brand.' McCharlie, indeed.

The Guardian (Vulliamy, 18 January 2015)[31] continues:

> Which begs the question that *Charlie Hebdo*'s circle is asking: what have we to do with the leaders of Turkey, Qatar, Britain, Israel, the European Union? The cartoonists insist that *Charlie* is not and never was a vehicle for politicians to posture. Quite the reverse: *Charlie Hebdo* was described decades ago as '*bête et méchant*' — bad and naughty — and has revelled in the description ever since. Wednesday's defiant edition carried the subtitle: 'Irresponsible Journal'. *Charlie Hebdo* does not want to go the way of Che

---

[29]https://www.theguardian.com/media/2015/jan/18/charlie-hebdo-we-cant-let-this-change-our-cartoons-nor-will-it (Retrieved 13 August 2017).
[30]The survival issue.
[31]https://www.theguardian.com/media/2015/jan/18/charlie-hebdo-we-cant-let-this-change-our-cartoons-nor-will-it (Retrieved 13 August 2017).

Guevara or Bob Marley and become co-opted by the establishment. And this cannot logically happen, because as Willem says, there is one thing that no establishment, no dogma, religion or ideology, can bear: mockery. And this runs deep, through the history of mankind and power, especially in France.

Reflecting popular sentiment, *Time* (Linshi, 18 January 2015)[32] reported on a survey conducted by the French weekly newspaper *Le Journal du Dimanche*, which had found that over 57% of the French people were in favour of the Prophet Muhammad image being published even if 'some Muslims feel attacked or injured by the publication of cartoons of the Prophet Muhammad' (JDD, 15 January 2015).[33] Among the respondents in a sample of some 1000 French adults, 42% were against publication. The survey also found that women and people under 35 were the most sensitive to Muslim concerns (Linshi, 18 January 2015).

Although the survey does not represent a serious investigation of French public opinion, it does offer valuable insight into the controversy stirred up by *Charlie Hebdo* as a satirical newspaper and its publication policy, even among those who, in principle, were 'Je suis Charlie' and against the attacks.

Sadly enough, the *Charlie Hebdo* attacks were not the only or the last terror attack in France that year, but in fact the beginning of a series of atrocities. On 13 November of the same year, ISIL terrorists carried out a series of attacks on the Bataclan theatre, which was staging a heavy music concert that night; on the Stade de France where France were playing Germany in football and where President Hollande was watching the game; and on random restaurants in Paris. More than 130 people were killed and 350 injured. The massacre targeted ordinary people who were enjoying their weekend, and many of the victims, particularly in the Bataclan, were young adults. Again, there was a massive show of public mourning after the attacks both in Paris and around the world, including social media slogans such as 'Pray for Paris.'

---

[32]http://time.com/3672921/charlie-hebdo-prophet-muhammad-muslim-cartoon-poll/ (Retrieved 7 September 2017).
[33]http://www.lejdd.fr/Politique/Sondage-JDD-57-des-Francais-veulent-des-caricatures-mais-713532 (Retrieved 13 August 2017).

In Nice, on the evening of Bastille Day on 14 July 2016 (French National Day), another atrocity followed when a jihadist lorry driver ploughed into crowds walking along Promenade des Anglais, killing 86 people and injuring over 450. ISIL claimed responsibility for the attack.

Other terrorist attacks that followed (the *Charlie Hebdo* attack) in other Eurpoean countries and around the world include the Beirut attacks in 2015, the Orlando nightclub massacre in 2016, the Brussels bombings in 2016, the Berlin Christmas market attacks in 2016, the St. Petersburg metro attacks in 2017 and the Istanbul nightclub shooting in 2017.

In the wake of these attacks, shootings and bombings, all seen as part of the global succession of terrorist incidents, the *Charlie Hebdo* shootings in January 2015 have been interpreted and re-interpreted against the events that followed, and those that went before. As Robin Wagner-Pacifici (2017) puts it, to remember and to make sense of past events is not a closed entity, but it keeps changing as our present changes. In other words, we must remain reflective about the present from the vantage point of which we analyse the past.

An examination of the *Charlie Hebdo* attacks within the broader framework of media event theory shows that this event was constructed out of several incidents of high symbolic value, which were quickly condensed and mythologized around existing mnemonic patterns of interpretation (see Sonnevend, 2016; Zelizer, 2018). The event had many beginnings and was made sense of in an interpretive framework that extended far beyond the actual incidents during the days of the killings and their immediate aftermath. In this sense, the *Charlie Hebdo* attacks resemble those earlier disruptive media events of unexpected violence that have been discussed in rethinking media events since Daniel Dayan and Elihu Katz (1992) original idea of ceremonial events. One paradigmatic case in this rethinking has been that of the 9/11 attacks in the USA (see, e.g., Wagner-Pacifici, 2017). In the *Charlie Hebdo* attacks and on 9/11, the news media went into disaster marathon mode (e.g., Liebes, 1998), launching a continuous stream of reporting on the attacks and putting on hold its regular agenda. Both cases also saw a sharp and all-pervasive polarization between 'the West' and 'the rest' in the media coverage. One key difference between 9/11 and the *Charlie Hebdo* attacks has to do with the media environment. In the wake of the *Charlie Hebdo* attacks, the social media and its various actors played a fundamental role not only in shaping the narratives of the event, but also in accelerating the interaction and remediation between professional news media and social media. The circulation of Ahmed Merabet's death video in both the news media and social media is a model example of this type of hybridization in the *Charlie Hebdo* media event.

Furthermore, the main narrative in the *Charlie Hebdo* attacks was symbolized in the slogan 'Je suis Charlie', in both news and social media, which was typically connected with the Western and French republican values of freedom of expression and, especially in the case of France, the principle of laïcité. Massive emotional reactions prompted the worldwide circulation of this slogan and stimulated different types of counter-narratives, some of which were heavy with emotional undertones. In this condition the live reporting, an essential element in all media events, became dispersed in the *Charlie Hebdo* attacks and is best described as a multi-channel and multi-actor activity which expanded well beyond the boundaries of the national media event.

In the following three chapters, we describe more closely the interplay between the narrative elements of the *Charlie Hebdo* attacks and their hybridization in this media event. We begin by identifying the key actors and their hybrid interactions in this media event. We also examine what kind of affordances were activated in those interactions. We then move on to illustrate the hybridization of attention and how it shaped the narrative construction of the event when the video of Ahmed Merabet's death went viral. Next, we turn to the hybridization of affect in the *Charlie Hebdo* attacks and examine in empirical detail the mediatized ritualization of the death of certain victims (namely the cartoonists) and the emotions and related narratives associated with those media practices. In the last empirical chapter, we examine acceleration as a mode of hybrid media events. We explain how digital communication was speeded up on diverse media platforms by different actors in two hostage situations, and how the media circulation of those incidents shaped the narrative construction of the event.

Chapter 3

Actors and Affordances

Hybrid media events are constructed in a complex interplay between different actors and technologies that theoretically come together in the concept of affordance. In line with Bruno Latour's (2005) ideas, we take the view that it is possible for both human and non-human actors to possess agency in communicative networks. Human actors are both individual and collective, and include organizations and institutions, individuals representing institutions or elites, as well as individuals with no particular power or prestige. Non-human actors consist of technological properties and conditions within and through which interaction takes place in hybrid media events. All of these actors have agency in hybrid media events, although this agency is defined and constrained by institutional and social relationships as well as affordances.

Based on these starting points, our investigation in this chapter addresses the question of actors, agency and affordances via two dimensions: through Twitter and on Twitter. This means that as well as investigating how certain human actors operate on Twitter, say by tweeting, retweeting, liking, replying and mentioning other actors, we also consider the role of non-human actors such as Twitter itself and its technological properties in the construction of a hybrid media event. Agency on Twitter and the agency of Twitter is enabled by affordances that can be defined as action possibilities that come into existence in encounters between actors, technology and the social (cf. Faraj & Azad, 2012). Although all objects and artefacts have affordances, the configuration of distance and proximity between actors in today's media events has been changed first and foremost by the properties associated with social media and affordances. Traditional theory of media events (Dayan & Katz, 1992), dating from the era of national broadcasting television and mass media, has it that media events take place outside the media, in 'remote locations' from which the media provide a channel for their transmission. Furthermore, in Dayan and Katz's understanding, events are organized and pre-planned outside the media, by public bodies with whom the media cooperate. In order to manage the technical complexity of production and to create expectations among viewers by means of promotion and advertising, broadcasters are given advance notice so that they can properly prepare for live broadcasts. Once all preparations are in place, the mass media forms a connection between the remote location and the audience in their living rooms. In this original theorization, then, the audience and other actors are left with the somewhat passive role of viewing the event at a distance, on their television sets (Dayan & Katz, 1992, pp. 5–9). Hybrid media events, by contrast, are created with and through the participation of different actors, including the audience that at times can also assume a producing role. The presence and involvement of a whole range of individual, non-human and collective actors in the construction of these events is made possible, first and foremost, by the technological and social affordances of the contemporary media environment.

Twitter and other microblogging sites represent an emblematic medium of this hybrid media environment. They bring together on the same platform both professional media, various organizations, political actors, ordinary users and the contents they have produced. As Dhiraj Murthy writes: 'Microblogging, more than many web spaces, is event driven. Organizing social life by events presents opportunities for everyday people and professional traditional media industries to tweet side-by-side' (Murthy, 2012, p. 1064). This resonates with Andrew Chadwick's account of hybrid media logic (2013), which is grounded in the interactions taking place across and between different older and newer media, that is, media professionals and those working outside the media field. Chadwick (2013, p. 21) continues: 'It also makes sense to move away from the idea of a relatively passive mass audience whose frames and perceptions are heavily shaped by a dominant media logic, and toward a model that foregrounds not only the increasingly diverse sources of audience frames and perceptions, but also the growing ability of some, though not all, activist "audience" members to play direct and concrete instrumental roles in the production of media content through their occasional decisive interventions.'

It is noteworthy then that there are marked asymmetries of power on Twitter. Twitter provides a platform that offers even non-media professionals at least the potential for attention. It has, however, been demonstrated in a number of studies that users who have attention, keep gaining attention. This is because actors with large numbers of followers can gain more engagement in the form of likes, shares or comments than users with only few followers.

3.1. Accounts and Hashtags

So what kind of agency does Twitter afford? In this chapter, we describe the affordances of Twitter's two key features, that is, accounts and hashtags. Actors are represented on Twitter through their accounts. By creating an account, actors can register a username that has the prefix @ and provide a short bio describing their Twitter persona. The presence and performance of actors on the platform materialize through that account.

One of the most important properties affording agency on Twitter is the hashtag. Hashtags were not an original feature of Twitter, but were adopted when web developer Chris Messina in 2007 suggested that the # sign be used to organize feeds according to topics of interest (Messina, 2007; Scott, 2015).

However, it took a moment of crisis for hashtags to find their way into wider use. In October 2007, web developer Nate Ritter was travelling around San Diego when he saw smoke pluming from an apparent fire. He switched on the television to learn more and to tell others on his blog. Soon he decided to turn to Twitter and started to use #SanDiegoFire. From that point on Ritter used the #SanDiegoFire hashtag for several days to share information about the fire (Pandell, 19 May 2017). This was the first example of a feed created around a certain theme that could be easily followed, joined and commented on by anyone interested. By 2009, the use of hashtags had been embraced by a sufficient number of users for Twitter to incorporate them in its platform (Scott, 2015).

From these origins, the hashtag feature was developed to create a hyperlink that allowed users to see all messages that included the same tag (Scott, 2015, p. 12). Hashtags thus function as metadata that link together related tweets and coordinate or promote content (Scott, 2015). In addition to these original functions, Kate Scott says that hashtags are nowadays also used to contextualize messages: '[H]ashtags have developed beyond their original search functionality to allow users to make certain contextual assumptions accessible to their readers and thus bridge the gap between the tweeter's cognitive environment and the potentially disparate cognitive environments of the readers' (Scott, 2015, p. 12). All Twitter users can now create a hashtag by adding the # sign before a certain string of characters, but hashtags are also used to join a conversation or to comment on an existing topic. Hashtags also allow users to follow in real time which topics are trending on Twitter, for instance, when large numbers of users are tweeting the same hashtag within a short period of time (Scott, 2015, p. 12). Instances of (terrorist) violence are typical situations when this Twitter property is used.

When viewed from the perspective of affordances, the most noteworthy point about hashtags is that they were innovated in a crisis setting by and for users. Their purpose was to make it easier to organize the contents of Twitter in a user-friendly way. These origins of hashtag usage are still echoed in the current affordances of hashtags, in that Twitter is often the social medium of choice at times of disruption, making it an important medium in hybrid media events (cf. Chapter 1).

As described earlier in the introduction, the concept of affordance is useful for purposes of exploring the interplay between the social and the material, that is human and non-human actors (cf. Faraj & Azad, 2012). The affordances of Twitter accounts and hashtags, then, have to do with the action possibilities and opportunities that emerge when actors are engaging with technology. In investigating these affordances, we have to take into consideration the things that the object (Twitter account or hashtag) performs, the user's perceptions, intentions and abilities, and the social context and the specifics of the situation. Analysis of affordances allows us to better understand hybrid media events, as technological properties bring together different actors not only on the same social media platform, but on the same feed. At the same time, this is the way in which human actors use these properties in their social contexts that make the hybrid media event.

In what follows, we first present an empirical examination of actors and affordances in the *Charlie Hebdo* attacks. This involves studying what kind of actors took part in the event on Twitter and analysing the dynamics between these actors. Second, we investigate what kind of agency the use of hashtags affords the actors in a hybrid media event. Third, we draw conclusions regarding relationships between the actors (i.e. proximity vs distance, stability vs constant change), and regarding self-amplification of hybrid media events.

Our Twitter dataset of 5.2 million tweets was collected using three search and filtering criteria, that is, search terms, time window and language. All tweets including any of the phrases 'Je suis Charlie', 'Je ne suis pas Charlie' or 'Je suis Ahmed' or any of hashtags #JeSuisCharlie, #JeNeSuisPasCharlie or #JeSuisAhmed that were sent during 7−16 January 2015 and written in either English, French or Arabic were included in the data (see Chapter 1).

3.2.   The Anatomy of the *Charlie Hebdo* Attacks on Twitter

The mediated action of the *Charlie Hebdo* attacks took off very rapidly on Twitter, most prominently around the hashtag #JeSuisCharlie. As described in Chapter 2, it was no more than some 20 minutes after the attacks had started at 11:30 a.m. that the French journalist and artist following the news in the media, Joachim Roncin from the *Stylist Magazine*, decided to comment on the news by creating a visual slogan or meme 'Je suis Charlie' on Twitter. Consisting of black, grey and white elements, the meme encapsulated the event in a recognizable visual scene (cf. Sonnevend, 2016). The word Charlie appeared in the same font as on the cover of the *Charlie Hebdo* magazine, while the black square background offered references to death, funerals and mourning. The message conveyed by the image turned immediately into a hashtag that flamed globally: #JeSuisCharlie became a trending topic and rapidly became one of the most tweeted hashtags once the news about the attacks began to spread. It was tweeted 6500 times in a minute and featured in 3.4 million tweets in a 24-hour period (Whitehead, 9 January 2015).[1]

Twitter users all over the world took part in constructing the hybrid media event by using the hashtag. A Twitter heat map created by Simon Rogers[2] neatly visualizes the temporal and spatial distribution of #JeSuisCharlie in the first two days after the attacks (7–8 January 2015). The animation is based on a world map where #JeSuisCharlie tweets are shown as lights. The first few lights appear in France and in neighbouring Spain, Portugal, Belgium, the Netherlands and the United Kingdom, and then along the east and west coasts of the USA. But within just a few hours, the whole of Europe, the USA, Canada's capital area, Latin America, the east coast of Brazil, South Africa, India, Japan, the Australian Capital Territory and New Zealand are all flashing white, stating #JeSuisCharlie.

There were also several remakes of #JeSuisCharlie. Produced by 1.8 million separate accounts, the most common variations of in a total of 5.2 million tweets were #JeSuisAhmed ('I am Ahmed'), #NousSommesCharlie ('We are all Charlie') and #JeNeSuisPasCharlie ('I am not Charlie'). Other hashtags used to tag messages related to the attacks included #CharlieHebdo, #Paris, #ParisShooting and #France (Figure 3.1).

---

[1]http://www.telegraph.co.uk/news/worldnews/europe/france/11336879/Paris-Charlie-Hebdo-attack-Je-Suis-Charlie-hashtag-one-of-most-popular-in-Twitter-history.html (Retrieved 23 October 2017).
[2]https://srogers.carto.com/viz/123be814-96bb-11e4-aec1-0e9d821ea90d/embed_map (Retrieved 30 October 2017).

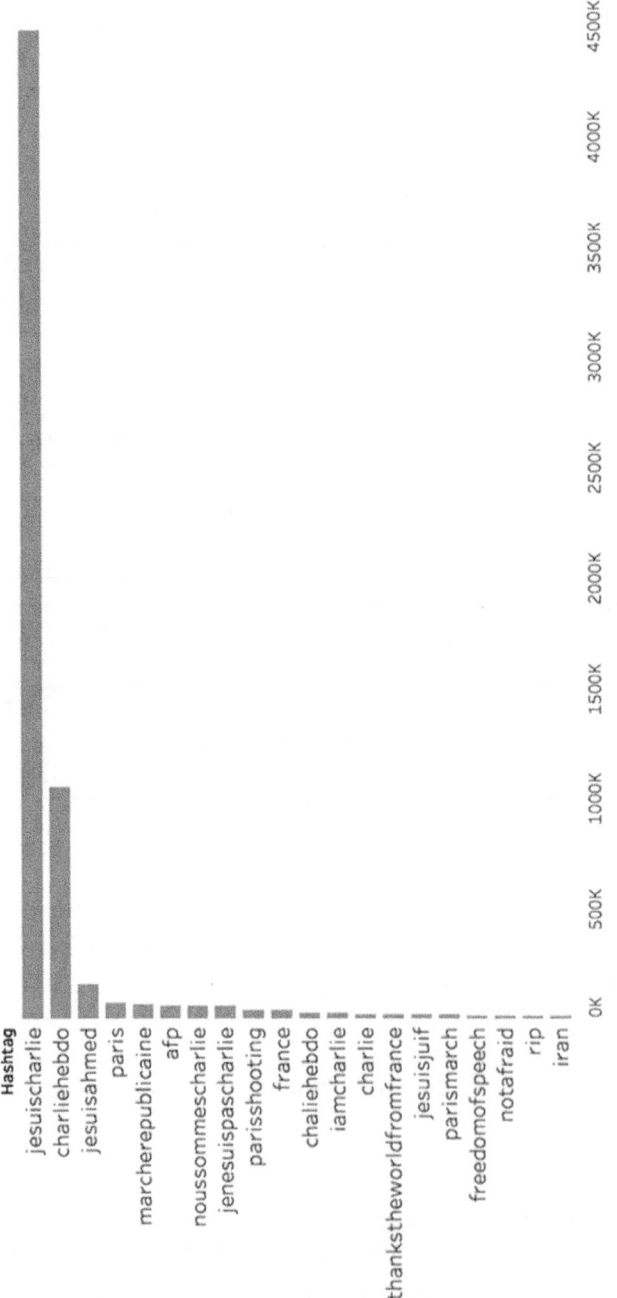

Figure 3.1:   Top 20 Most Used Hashtags in Twitter Messages Posted on the *Charlie Hebdo* Attacks.

3.2.1. Actors

In order to gain a better understanding of the dynamics, activities and variety of the actors involved in creating the hybrid media event around the *Charlie Hebdo* attacks, we have used computational methods to analyse the data in several ways.[3]

We wanted to find out which accounts were most prominent and active and which of them gained the most engagement and visibility in terms of mentions and retweets (Table 3.1). The top 100 of these most engaged accounts are a very heterogeneous group, as is typical of the hybrid media environment (cf. Chadwick, 2013). Based on our analysis, the actors can be classified into eight partly overlapping groups. In the following, the groups are not listed according to their size order, but instead according to their status and function in this hybrid media event:

1. The targets of the attack are represented by the Twitter accounts of the *Charlie Hebdo* magazine and emergency physician Patrick Pelloux, who had written articles for *Charlie Hebdo* since 2004. Pelloux was not in the newspaper's offices at the time of the shootings, but arrived soon after and provided first aid for his colleagues.
2. French cities, officials and politicians, such as of Paris and Toulouse, Prime Minister Manuel Valls and French police special forces Gendarmerie Nationale (GIGN).
3. Celebrities including well-known writers, musicians, internet personalities and actors, such as Salman Rushdie, Michéle Laroque, Justin Timberlake, Ellen DeGeneres and Jared Leto.
4. Social media giants are represented by Twitter and YouTube.
5. Individual media professionals, such as freelance copywriters, youtubers, PR and communication professionals, graphic designers,

---

[3]Our investigation uses a combination of computational, visual and social network analyses, which provide four complementary viewpoints on the actors. First, we have identified the most active tweeters in the dataset by counting the number of tweets sent by each actor. Second, we have identified the actors whose tweets received the most engagement and, in practice, visibility in the form of retweets. Third, we have applied a social network analysis (SNA) approach to study the network of interactions between actors to see how individual actors are connected on mentions and replies. This allowed us to identify the actors receiving the most mentions. Fourth, we have further analysed the social network in order to identify the most prestigious actors in the network by applying network metrics PageRank that takes into account both direct and indirect connections.

journalists tweeting from their personal accounts, illustrators and cartoonists.

6. Newer media companies, such as American internet media company Buzzfeed, which mainly tracks social media and entertainment, and Happie's, a French social media humour channel.

7. Ordinary Twitter users.

8. Professional media are represented by both international and French national media outlets, such as Agence France-Presse (AFP), one of the world's oldest news agencies; *Le Figaro*, a daily morning newspaper founded in 1826; *The New Yorker* magazine, a weekly magazine founded in 1925; *The Independent*, a British online newspaper; Europe 1, a French live radio station; *L'Équipe*, a French daily sports newspaper; *New York Magazine*, an American biweekly magazine; the British Broadcasting Corporation (BBC); Cable News Network (CNN); and BFMTV, a 24-hour rolling news channel based in France.

Table 3.1: Top 20 Users with the Largest Number of Retweets.

	Actor	Retweets Sum	Followers	Tweets
1	HappiesFr	43,422	1,431,486	3
2	Aboujahjah	39,119	8983	6
3	Afpfr	38,062	1,768,874	231
4	Le_Figaro	32,585	1,939,233	226
5	Cyrilhanouna	29,287	3,235,200	1
6	TheMagnusShaw	21,087	2326	13
7	Independent	17,308	1,800,374	41
8	GossipRoomOff	16,918	153,338	41
9	Paris	15,862	1,039,403	32
10	Nashgrier	15,862	5,424,028	1
11	SaraAssaf	15,335	22,604	11
12	Bipartisanism	15,010	202,519	79
13	AFPphoto	14,903	61,318	31
14	NewYorker	14,118	6,207,259	4
15	LucilleClerc	14,022	5762	2
16	Itele	13,913	692,850	126
17	mohamedbouhafsi	13,373	88,385	1
18	MicheleLaroque	12,353	105,661	26
19	BBCBreaking	12,253	21,498,118	8
20	sturdyAlex	12,137	32,070	17

3.2.2. Dynamics

The dynamics that make these groups stand out from the crowd of 1.8 million users in terms of their visibility and engagement can be traced to five interconnected aspects:

1. Actor's involvement with the case.
2. Actor's fame.
3. Stickiness of content.
4. Structure and practices of social media.
5. Self-amplification of hybrid media event.

First, visibility on Twitter was achieved by those actor groups who were directly involved with the case, that is the targets of the attack and French cities, officials and politicians. The *Charlie Hebdo* Twitter account is mentioned because the magazine and its staff were the intended target of the massacre and the victims whose demise sparked the out-pourings of shock and grief. Both the breaking news and tributes circulating on Twitter therefore often mentioned the magazine's username @Charlie_Hebdo_. Writer and physician Patrick Pelloux was also mentioned, as he was one of the surviving staff members. Pelloux appeared in public the day after the attack on Thursday 8 January, emphasizing that his dead colleagues had fought racism and that he felt no hate against Muslims, referring to the politicized discussion around the attack. The interview was arranged by French news channel iTélé (currently CNews), one of the most popular news channels in France. Other media then shared clips of the interview, greatly expanding its exposure (e.g., *Le Monde*, 8 January 2015a, 2015b).[4] Together with the magazine's artistic director Rénald Luzier, pen name Luz, Pelloux thus became a symbolic anchorage of attention and voice for *Charlie Hebdo* for a moment.

The other group of French cities, officials and politicians mentioned on Twitter were the city of Paris as the site of the event, and the city of Toulouse, which hosted vast solidarity demonstrations. Manuel Valls, French Prime Minister at the time, was mentioned in tweets as he, together with President Hollande and the Minister for the Interior, was charged with the political management of the conflict. It was

---

[4]http://www.lemonde.fr/actualite-medias/video/2015/01/08/charlie-hebdo-l-emotion-de-patrick-pelloux-urgentiste-et-chroniqueur_4551679_3236.html (Retrieved 23 October 2017).

Prime Minister Valls who appeared in public to explain how the French nation will react to the attacks. The National Gendarmerie (GIGN) also gained attention on Twitter. GIGN was responsible for killing the perpetrators after a massive security operation. The unit continued to post news and statements on Twitter and Facebook throughout the crisis, and the number of people following their account increased sharply (Ehrhard & Garrier, 2015). All these actors were integrally involved in the event in the roles of targets of the attack, victims, sites of the event and political and operational management of the conflict and these roles earned them significant exposure in Twittersphere.

The second dynamics driving the authority of Twitter actors relates to the issue of fame. Some of these users, most notably celebrities, attract such large numbers of followers on Twitter that every tweet they send out generates tremendous engagement. American comedian and television host Ellen DeGeneres, for instance, tweeted on Thursday 8 January: 'My heart is with the city of Paris #JeSuisCharlie.' Although this tweet from @TheEllenShow account may be considered a rather generic expression of solidarity, it prompted a strong reaction among her followers and was soon retweeted over 8500 times (Figure 3.2). Other Twitter users with large following also passed on this message of solidarity. This was the case when Gossip Room, a newer French lifestyle and entertainment company, translated the tweet into French and mentioned Ellen DeGeneres's name on Thursday 8 January 2015:

> @TheEllenShow 'Mon Coeur est avec la ville de Paris' #JeSuisCharlie

This again increased the visibility and engagement of @TheEllenShow. American pop star Justin Timberlake commented on the event on Thursday 8 January in a tweet that said, 'Pray for those families who lost loved ones AND the people senseless enough to commit this travesty. #JeSuisCharlie.'[5] The message was retweeted almost 6000 times in a short space of time.

The third dynamics driving authority on Twitter is the stickiness of content. Here, it is the content of the tweet that attracts attention, though the original number of account followers can be considered low. This category comprises individual media professionals, newer media companies, ordinary people and, to some extent, professional media. The most retweeted message in our dataset is from the French media company

---

[5]Emphasis in the original.

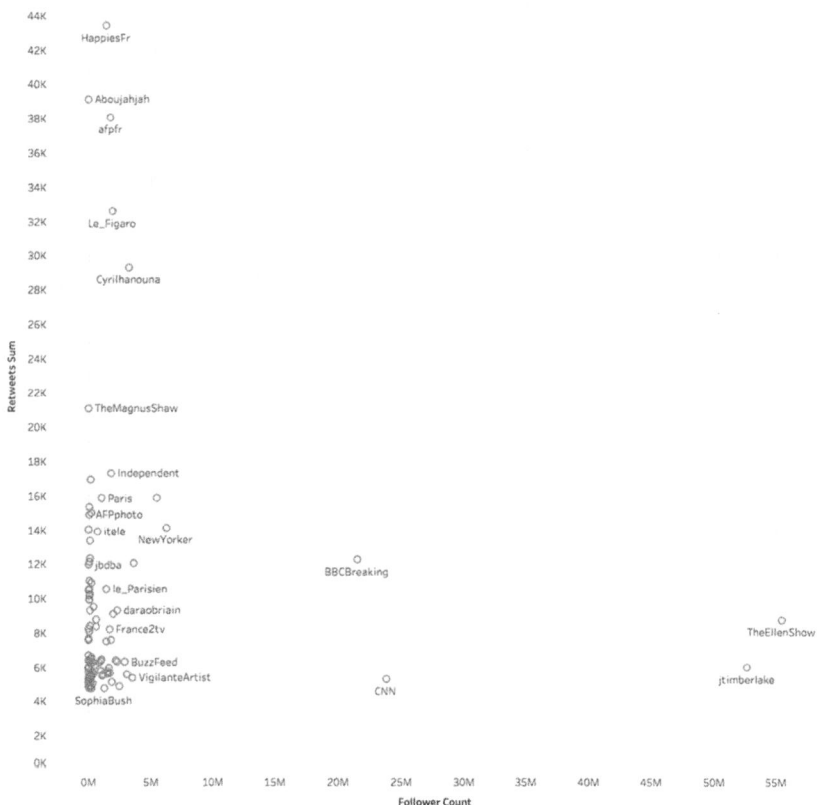

Figure 3.2: Scatter Plot of the Relationship between Number of Twitter Users' Followers and the Numbers of Retweets They Received.

Happie's (Figure 3.2). It contains an image of a crowd carrying candles and has the caption, 'Ils voulaient mettre la France à genoux, ils l'ont mise debout' ('They wanted to put France on its knees, they made it stand up'). Individual media professionals are a highly influential group in our dataset, posting many of the tweets that gained the most engagement. Freelance copywriter Magnus Shaw tweeted on Wednesday 7 January 2015, a picture of a crying Charlie Brown with the caption, 'Je suis Charlie'. The tweet itself says, 'A terrible day for all cartoonists. #JeSuisCharlie.' It drew more than 21,000 retweets. In addition, there are many more elaborate drawings commenting on the event, such as a picture of three pens drawn by illustrator Lucille Clerc: one intact pen represents yesterday, another broken pen represents today, and a third pen, in two pieces but with two sharp tips, represents tomorrow. The caption says, 'Break one, a thousand will rise.' The attention captured by this insightful illustration was partly due to a misunderstanding. The image was posted on a popular but unverified Instagram account of the famous graffiti artist Banksy, and therefore initially attributed to this street artist. On Thursday 8 January, however, Banksy's representative confirmed the image was not Banksy's work (Selby, 8 January 2015),[6] and the spotlight of attention turned to Lucille Clerc. Her tweet generated nearly 14,000 mentions. As can be seen from the examples above, this type of content is typically affective, and the attraction is created through symbolic expressions (the Eiffel tower, the pencil) or by appealing to emotions or expressions of emotion (crying Charlie Brown).

In the group of ordinary people, a good example is provided by user Sara Assaf, who commented on the event several times on Twitter. On Thursday 8 January 2015, she posted a tweet containing two photographs of the solidarity demonstrations with the caption, 'Paris now. In all its splendor. #JeSuisCharlie #CharlieHebdo.' One image shows a crowd of people carrying a 'Not afraid' sign, another shows people gathered around candlelit stairs.

Interestingly, among the most retweeted messages is one that does not say #JeSuisCharlie, but #JeSuisAhmed. Dyab Abou Jahjah, in a middle-ground position between an individual media professional and ordinary user, tweeted on Thursday 8 January 2015:

> I am not Charlie, I am Ahmed the dead cop. Charlie ridiculed my faith and culture and I died defending his right to do so. #JesuisAhmed

This tweet was shared over 35,500 times and put Ahmed Merabet at the centre of attention. This tweet resonated especially among Muslims in France.

The fourth dynamics of visibility in Twittersphere relates to the technological structures and social practices of sharing in social media. YouTube provides a case in point. The video sharing site was soon inundated with videos relating to the attacks, some featuring news and many paying tribute to the victims. Our data show that as users shared these YouTube videos on Twitter, YouTube as an actor was

---

[6]http://www.independent.co.uk/news/people/banksys-striking-illustrated-response-to-the-charlie-hebdo-attack-9964198.html (Retrieved 23 October 2017).

automatically mentioned in that tweet. One video filmed on Thursday 8 January 2015 in Trafalgar Square, London, shows more than 100 musicians playing a tribute song for the victims. This video was shared on Twitter by user @Benoitdx9, bringing a mention to YouTube:

Je Suis Charlie: http://t.co/B2uSIEm7hh via@YouTube

The fifth dynamic is related to the self-amplifying tendency of hybrid media events and sheds light on the interrelations between human and non-human actors and the centrality of attention as a dimension in hybrid media events. As actors participate in the event through their comments and shares, they at once intensify the phenomenon on which they are commenting. This dynamic also serves to multiply the role of Twitter (Figure 3.3). As well as enabling the

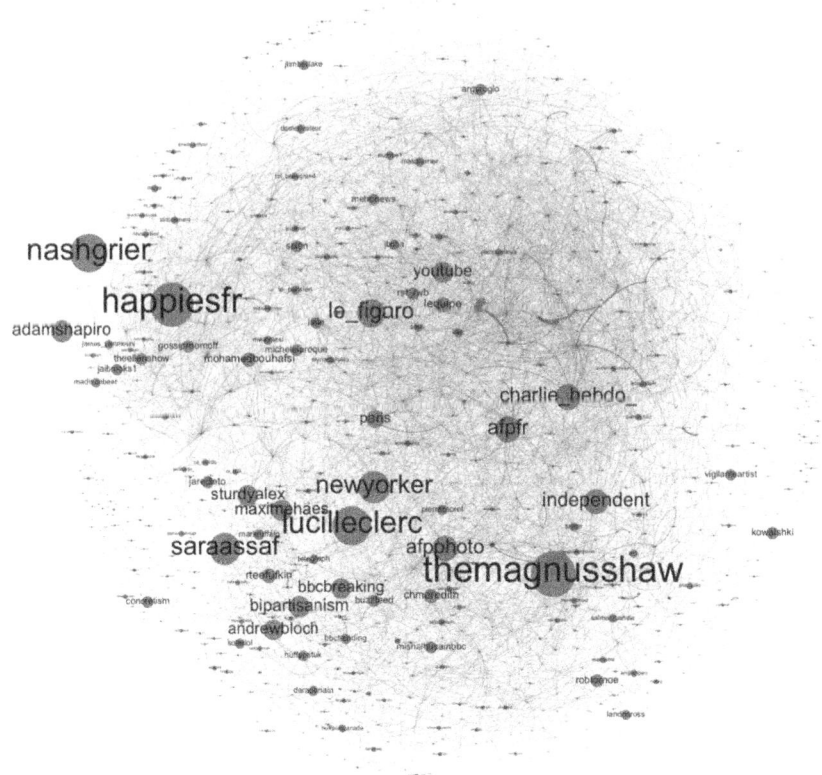

Figure 3.3: Network Visualization of the Most Authoritative Actors in the Twitter Data.

agency of human and institutional actors, Twitter also assumed agency of its own and became an actor among others. To put it simply, it was the popularity of #JeSuisCharlie that generated agency for Twitter. First, #JeSuisCharlie peaked as a trending topic on Twitter. This phenomenon was rapidly and recursively strengthened by professional media news, individual media professionals such as Simon Rogers who created a viral visualization, and ordinary people and celebrities who kept on tweeting #JeSuisCharlie. These tweets enhanced the volume of the hashtag and generated new stories about the 'most popular hashtag ever on @Twitter'. As these tweets commenting on a phenomenon happening on Twitter continued to circulate on the platform, they also time and again reinforced the role of @Twitter. As a result, Twitter ranks among the most visible actors in our dataset. This is the process through which the attention economy works, and how things become to be in the hybrid media environment. Through these processes, some things accumulate attention while others remain unseen and unnoticed (Table 3.2).

The visibility of traditional media is intertwined with all five dynamics mentioned above. The professional media were heavily involved with the case, as it had two constitutive roles in this hybrid media event. The attack against the *Charlie Hebdo* magazine was, firstly, an attack against a media outlet, and professional media were therefore closely involved with the case: symbolically, in their role of advocates of free speech, they were all the target. Secondly, professional media were involved in broadcasting the event, a role that is underlined in the original theory of media events (Dayan & Katz, 1992). Furthermore, some professional media have significant Twitter followings, echoing the fame and followers of celebrities. Also, as they have moved to align their operation with the logics of newer media, professional media have created technological structures that make it possible to share their contents on social media. Thus, the contents of professional media are now fluently shared on Twitter and YouTube. In addition, because of their particularly close involvement with the case, professional media commented on the event by creating sticky contents. For example, a tweet sent on Friday 9 January in which *The New Yorker* magazine released its cover for the week following the attacks gained massive engagement. The cover illustration combines the symbol of Paris and the symbol of the event in an illustration of the Eiffel Tower morphing into a pen as it peaks. Another attractive tweet was posted by AFP's photo department, showing a photo of its editorial staff holding A4 prints with the 'Je suis Charlie' slogan.

Table 3.2: How Twitter Actors Mention Twitter in Their Tweets.

Actor	Retweets	Content
amazingmap	1976.0	WORLD : #JeSuisCharlie Most popular hashtag EVER in @twitter history http://t.co/WjWp3dO1l7
cnn	1778.0	#JeSuisCharlie has become one of the most popular hashtags in @Twitter's history http://t.co/QWuM1wo2dW via @CNNMoney http://t.co/XB6cuyfZsJ
domdelport	1709.0	WORLD : #JeSuisCharlie Most popular hashtag ever in @twitter history http://t.co/yBiMTN1omj http://t.co/mju44rRgiB
marksluckie	818.0	#JeSuisCharlie hashtag going up @twitter HQ http://t.co/Xu7QovFHLU
cnnmoney	497.0	#JeSuisCharlie has now become one of @twitter's most popular hashtags http://t.co/1IP6xc0Hgb http://t.co/AXxT4eFknA
julies	278.0	Les bureaux de @Twitter à San Francisco immortalisent #JeSuisCharlie http://t.co/AClFc1l1Ki
socialsecretuk	234.0	At 6500 tweets per minute #JeSuisCharlie is most popular hashtag in @twitter history. This is the map. http://t.co/ncQE4xYJub
moicelestia	205.0	Pourquoi le hastag #JeSuisKouachi est toujours permis?!? WHY @twitter ?! #JeSuisCharlie http://t.co/p9d1bWZF1p
malasqalani	193.0	WORLD : #JeSuisCharlie Most popular hashtag ever in @twitter history https://t.co/Nj1fpfP8wp http://t.co/3NayLk3z1z http://t.co/yTigioyXij
benjaminramm	189.0	Wow. RT @amazingmap: WORLD: #JeSuisCharlie Most popular hashtag EVER in @twitter history http://t.co/Rgibxqe8AX

Lastly, professional media also took part in the amplification of the hybrid media event and at once established their own central role in the event. CNN's programme OutFront account, for instance, tweeted on Saturday 10 January:

> Why #JeSuisCharlie has now become one of @twitter's most popular hashtags: http://t.co/2qj7hF4hYB @CNN @CNNMoney http://t.co/jXgU3vMUoi

In this tweet, professional media actor @outfrontcnn mentions two other professional media accounts, @CNN and @CNNMoney. All three belong to the same traditional media corporation. References by one media to others will obviously contribute to elevate this group to the very top of the whole crowd of actors.

Although the hybrid media event around the *Charlie Hebdo* attacks was first and foremost created by and through the actors and dynamics described above, our computational analysis also highlighted other contributing phenomena within the digital media environment. Our dataset includes several accounts that sent out thousands of tweets within a very short period of time. In many cases, these were probably bots running on Twitter, either repeating the same tweet over and over, or just collecting any tweets under trending hashtags. However, although the logic of these non-human actors might seem obscure, they were involved in co-constructing the event along with other Twitter users.

Our computational analysis has provided new insight into the dynamics and roles of the actors most prominently involved in making the 'Je suis Charlie' statement. However, there still remain several smaller but nonetheless significant features of the *Charlie Hebdo* attacks that this analysis has not yet touched upon. Our examination of the affordances of hashtags, therefore, turns now to digital ethnography and to tracing the opposite statement, which was intended to express support for the perpetrators of the attack.

3.3.   Tracing #JeSuisKouachi: Affordances of Hashtags

Whereas the #JeSuisCharlie dataset represents the mass solidarity aroused by the attack on the *Charlie Hebdo* offices, #JeSuisKouachi represents a completely opposite view on the issue. The hashtag referring to the perpetrators Saïd and Chérif Kouachi appeared on Twitter's trending topics list by Friday 9 January 2015. At that time, typing the words 'je suis' on Twitter automatically brought up the suggestion 'Kouachi'. On that Friday morning on 9 January, French Minister of the Interior Bernard Cazeneuve said that users of several social media sites had reported more than 3700 messages sent in support of the *Charlie Hebdo* terror attacks (Sulzer, 10 January 2015).[7] According to the social media analysis tool Topsy, #JeSuisKouachi had been used 21,230 times by Saturday morning, 10 January; by Tuesday 13 January, that number had risen to 38,231. Although these figures are of course very low compared to those recorded for #JeSuisCharlie, the use of #JeSuisKouachi received strong public condemnation. French Prime Minister Manuel Valls pointed the finger at those supporting terror attacks and said, 'It is clear from what we see happening on the internet that the evil runs deeper' (Sulzer, 10 January 2015). These messages created an atmosphere of moral panic and prompted one of the socialist deputies to issue a statement in which he encouraged internet users to blow the whistle on anyone using the hashtag #JeSuisKouachi, adding that supporting terrorism should 'carry a punishment of seven years of imprisonment' (Sulzer, 10 January 2015).

Some of the early Twitter feeds around #JeSuisKouachi, apparently sent by Arabic-speaking Twitter users, said 'I am a Muslim and Kouachi represents me. #JeSuisKouachi.' Another message read: 'This is the beginning, open your accounts, we want to die we will kill you and we will take our historic revenge. #JeSuisKouachi.' However, by the time that the news media began to report on these tweets, suspicions had been raised about their source. *L'Express* reported on Saturday 10 January 2015 that it seemed many of the messages had actually been written by people with extreme-right sympathies. This observation is borne out by our data which indicate that the hashtag was soon hijacked. Hashtag hijacking refers to the use of a certain hashtag for completely different purposes than the one originally intended. Hashtag hijacking is also associated with the generation of counter-narratives and reframing of the original message (e.g., Jackson & Foucault Welles, 2015).

The tweets around #JeSuisKouachi were mainly written in French, but also English, Dutch and Arabic. Although it probably started out as a pro-terrorism statement, the hashtag eventually became a channel for

---

[7]http://www.lexpress.fr/actualite/societe/les-reseaux-sociaux-servent-ils-a-faire-l-apolo-gie-des-attentats_1639336.html (Retrieved 23 October 2017).

heated and often vulgar debate around the relationship between terrorism and Islam. Accounts using #JeSuisKouachi were not run by professional or new media actors or celebrities, but by ordinary unfamous Twitter users, or fake accounts set up by individuals or groups. For this reason, they cannot be categorized in the same way as in the case of #JeSuisCharlie. They can, however, be divided into six categories that show interesting internal dynamics: (1) Those who vehemently opposed the use of #JeSuisKouachi. These actors also resisted the fact that anyone could identify with the Kouachi brothers and in fact with Muslims in general. (2) This group was the exact opposite to the first one, in that these users were keen to emphasize the humanity and peaceful nature of Islam and Muslims. (3) Those who bemoaned the original purpose of the hashtag. (4) This group challenged the previous one: their argument was that users bemoaning the original purpose of the hashtag were just hypocrites, in that they would only allow and accept free speech for the select few. (5) A group of informers who were interested in reviewing the various incidents related to *Charlie Hebdo* and who therefore used #JeSuisKouachi, among many other event-related hashtags. And finally, (6) those who used the hashtag for their own random purposes, which do not necessarily even relate to the *Charlie Hebdo* attacks: they were just using the hashtag to gain attention — this was after all a trending issue.

Twitter users who were opposed to the hashtag (the first group) were motivated to create confrontation between Christians and Muslims, between West and East. They did this by referring, for example, to Frankish statesman and military leader Charles Martel, who has been framed and credited as the warrior who stanched the Muslim expansion into Western Europe in the eighth century. In fact, Charles Martel is a well-known iconic figure in fascist and far-right movements in France and other Western countries, and was commonly mentioned by the far right following the *Charlie Hebdo* attacks (Rehman, 2016). Importantly, the founder of the French Front National Party, Jean-Marie Le Pen also stated 'Je suis Charlie Martel' after the attacks (*The Huffington Post France*, 9 January 2015).[8] The slogan was used by the first group of Twitter actors in the form of #JeSuisCharlieMartel. Another purpose of these messages was to bring disgrace upon Muslims by posting caricatures of the Prophet Muhammad and the 72 virgins of Paradise. Furthermore, these tweets contained distasteful images with direct

---

[8]http://www.huffingtonpost.fr/2015/01/09/jean-marie-le-pen-front-national-charlie-martel-hebdo-tweet-declarations_n_6443248.html (Retrieved 2 November 2017).

references to homosexuality, penetrations, interference with animals and paedophilia. In many cases, these provocative images were shared from troll-like accounts such as @Alkhalifa775 several times in succession, so that for a short period the feed was filled with the same image.

Users proclaiming the peaceful intentions of Islam, on the other hand, attached to their tweets images of parts of the Quran, which condemns violence in all its forms, and pictures of terror victims from different ethnic backgrounds. Users who bemoaned the use of #JeSuisKouachi often appealed to Twitter that it should not provide a platform for the expression of terrorist sympathies. Finally, users who underlined the hypocrisy of those rejecting any identification with terrorists, shared images of atrocities committed by Western people. These messages created narratives reminding people that Christianity as a whole is not blamed for the crimes of some Christians, which is precisely what is done in the case of the Muslim population and a few Islamist perpetrators.

It is noteworthy that messages serving the pro-Kouachi purpose of the hashtag are almost completely absent from our dataset. It is possible that either Twitter or the users themselves have deleted such messages, as they only exist as fragments in the feed. These fragments are mainly visible as screenshots posted by another account.

Overall then, the motives for tweeting #JeSuisKouachi varied widely. However, although only very few of these users wanted to support the perpetrators, the mere use of the hashtag boosted its prominence in the hybrid media environment. The irony of the affordance of hashtags is that users who either condemned the message 'I am Kouachi' or who felt that people should refrain from giving exposure to terrorism, only added to the visibility of 'Je suis Kouachi' by addressing their comments to this particular discussion and tagging their tweets #JeSuisKouachi.

3.4. Hybrid Media Events Amplify Themselves

Hybrid media events of terrorist violence are created by multiple actors in digital communication networks. Twitter is one of the key interfaces where different voices and narratives encounter each other in the channels formed around hashtags. Our empirical investigation of Twitter illustrates how the constellation between actors in hybrid media events is in constant flux. Importantly, the dynamics taking place on Twitter reduces the distance between different actors and affords a possibility for a variety of users to gain attention in hybrid media events.

Furthermore, Twitter's key property of hashtags affords different things for different actors, depending on their perceptions. While some actors create and use hashtags to demonstrate solidarity, others create and use them to support the perpetrators. New media, for their part, use hashtags to spread their news about the topic. Hashtags can also be hijacked for purposes opposite to the original meanings. It can be argued then that Twitter brings a certain element of unpredictability to hybrid media events. Trolls and bots, for example, may disturb hybrid media events in many unpredictable ways. This said, while the roles of actors in television era media events were rather stable, the actor roles of and in hybrid media events are constantly moving and changing. In short, the intensified communication between diverse actors in hybrid media events tends to amplify the event itself. Every piece of information, every comment and mention that relates to the event magnifies its existence. From this point of view, it makes no difference whether the comment or post is a deep analysis of the incidents, an appeal to stop drawing attention to the perpetrators or a bot repeating a certain hashtag. All these communicative actions intensify communication of, in and about the event and by so doing amplify its hybrid reality.

Chapter 4

Attention

In this chapter, our focus is on the workings of attention in the *Charlie Hebdo* attacks, particularly on how the circulation and accumulation of attention contributed to the hybridization of this global media event. As discussed earlier in the introduction, we argue that all media events today are largely about a contest for attention, and that the hybrid media environment is based on the logic of the attention economy (Davenport & Beck, 2001). Attention tracking — counting the number of clicks, likes, shares, etc. — has become a major means of media revenue generation, and therefore, all those involved in media events are affected by this logic. Not only mainstream media houses and professional journalists, but also politicians, perpetrators and ordinary media users are keen to attract attention and to try to manage that attention for their own purposes. Attention is most typically accumulated and directed through the circulation of media representations such as news, memes, visuals, texts and videos. Affective and visual contents tend to command attention more easily than neutral contents, and therefore, they are more popular subjects in the circulation of media events (see also Papacharissi, 2015). The following illustrates the workings of attention in the *Charlie Hebdo* attacks by examining the death of Muslim police officer Ahmed Merabet and the news media and social media halo that followed his death. What we want to show is how the attention around Merabet shaped the meaning making and narrativization of *Charlie Hebdo* as a media event and how it was applied to moderate the controversy between the different parties in the event, namely the 'Western' victims and the Muslim perpetrators.

4.1. Ahmed Merabet's Death Goes Viral

Ahmed Merabet, a Muslim of Algerian origin, was in his forties at the time of his sudden death. He was shot dead by the Kouachi brothers near the *Charlie Hebdo* offices, while he was patrolling the neighbourhood. The shooting was to become the most visible testimony to the killers' violence.

Having first been gunned down to the ground, Merabet was then executed by a shot to the head. *The Guardian* (Burke, 8 January 2015; Penketh, 8 January 2015)[1] describes Merabet's last moments as follows:

> As he falls to the pavement groaning in pain and holding up an arm as though to protect himself, the second gunman moves forward and asks the policeman: 'Do you want to kill us?' Merabet replies: 'Non, c'est bon, chef' ['No, it's OK mate']. The terrorist then shoots him in the head.

Merabet's death received huge public interest primarily because of the visual evidence that became available. The shooting was captured on the mobile phone of an accidental bystander, Jordi Mir, who was at home sending an e-mail when he was interrupted by the sound of gunshots and drawn to the window. At first he had no idea what he was filming; the thought of a bank robbery crossed his mind. When the police arrived on the scene, Mir handed over his amateur video and then posted the 42-second clip on Facebook. He soon regretted this and decided to remove the video from his Facebook page of 2500 friends just 15 minutes later — but was no longer able to prevent its circulation in the digital media. According to the Associated Press (Satter, 11 January 2015),[2] someone had picked up the video and uploaded it on YouTube. Less than an hour after taking down the video, Jordi saw it being broadcast on television.

This was the first step and prerequisite for the symbolic importance that Ahmed Merabet's death came to play in the *Charlie Hebdo* attacks. Without a circulating video clip of his killing, the case would have gained much less attention. This demonstrates the dynamics of attention in hybrid media events: something only comes to existence in circulation. If there is no documentation of an event, circulation is impossible. Jordi's graphic clip went viral and began to circulate in the social media and on the online sites of various news media, including *The New York Times*, Reuters and *The Guardian*. On the day after the execution, the picture of Merabet being shot in the head appeared on the front page of *The Times*, *The Daily Telegraph*, *The New York Times*, the *Daily Mirror*, *The Sun*, the *Daily Mail* and other newspapers. The Associated

---

[1]https://www.theguardian.com/world/2015/jan/08/ahmed-merabet-mourned-charlie-hebdo-paris-attack (Retrieved 6 October 2017).
[2]https://www.apnews.com/5e1ee93021b941629186882f03f1bb79 (Retrieved 10 October 2017).

Press (11 January 2015) describes the reactions in the world news media as follows:

> The video unleashed a worldwide wave of revulsion. British tabloids described it as 'shocking' and 'sickening.' France's *Le Figaro* ran a still from the footage on its front page over a caption which read 'War.' CNN's Randi Kaye called it 'an unforgettable image forever associated with this horrible attack.'

The video showed the actual killing of Ahmed Merabet and the perpetrators fleeing. It provided powerful, emotionally laden visual testimony of the execution and shrank the distance between the actual death scene, the people involved in the event and the audience, intensifying the attention around Merabet. The news media began to narrate Merabet's life and tragic death. Jordi Mir's video clip provided authentic, first-hand eyewitness evidence, which seemed to fit in well with the mediatized disaster logic of the news and social media.

Ahmed Merabet on News Covers.[3]

---

[3]Photograph copyright Paula Kallio.

4.2.   The Media Makes Merabet an Ideal Victim

The news media created several storylines around Merabet's life. They said he had grown up in Livry-Gargan in the north-eastern suburbs of Paris and graduated from the local lycée in 1995. *Paris Match* (Lallement, 23 January 2015)[4] reported that Merabet's father Kaddour had migrated to France in 1955 and his mother Houria in 1962. He was said to have fulfilled his responsibility as the family's eldest son after his father's death and begun to look after his mother and siblings. Like many other newspapers, *Le Figaro* (De Mareschal, 13 January 2015)[5] portrayed Ahmed and his family as good, hard-working citizens. Ahmed was praised as a devoted officer who worked hard to gain promotion in the police force (Graham-Harrison, 10 January 2015).[6] Malek, Ahmed's brother, described Ahmed in a *Guardian* news story (10 January 2015):

> 'Through sheer determination he had recently passed the CID entrance exam and was due to come off the beat. His colleagues describe him as a man of action who was passionate about his job,' Malek said.

In other words, the news reporting on Merabet established him as an ideal victim (Greer, 2004) in this media event. It is typical of media texts to narrativize disruptive events in terms of heroes and villains, victims and attackers. It is also typical that perpetrators are portrayed as outsiders to the community/society, while the ideal victims and heroes belong to 'us'.

Merabet was portrayed as one of 'us', despite his roots. It was said that he had come from a relatively humble Maghreb Muslim background in one of the banlieux of Paris. He had nonetheless carved out a life for himself as a son, partner, brother and respected colleague. He died defending the very people who offended his religion. His tragic fate was to die just one day before he was due to be promoted to detective, which would have brought him out of the streets. To sum up then, the news media made Merabet a tragic masculine Muslim hero, who provided a dramatic contrast to the killers (who were portrayed as bad

---

[4]http://www.parismatch.com/Actu/Societe/Son-itineraire-exemplaire-Ahmed-Merab et-695190 (Retrieved 10 October 2017).
[5]http://www.lefigaro.fr/actualite-france/2015/01/13/01016-20150113ARTFIG00418-mus ulmans-juifs-et-policiers-pleurent-ahmed-merabet.php (Retrieved 10 October 2017).
[6]https://www.theguardian.com/world/2015/jan/10/charlie-hebdo-policeman-murder-ahmed-merabet (Retrieved 10 October 2017).

Muslims). In other words, the news media narrativized his life into a heroic story of a good Muslim, who had not only adjusted to French society, but even internalized its values.

In the words of Malek, Ahmed's brother who became a prominent witness to his brother's character as a good Muslim and French citizen:

> 'My brother was Muslim and he was killed by two terror-
> ists, by two false Muslims,' he said. 'Islam is a religion of
> peace and love. As far as my brother's death is concerned
> it was a waste. He was very proud of the name Ahmed
> Merabet, proud to represent the police and of defending
> the values of the Republic — liberty, equality, fraternity.'
> (Graham-Harrison, 10 January 2015)[7]

Merabet's partner Morgane Ahmad also appeared in public to comment on Ahmed Merabet's fate. The family's message was to call for calm and unity, and their comments, statements and interviews were circulated from one news media platform to another. In the words of Morgane Ahmad:

> 'What the family and I want is for everyone to be united,
> we want everyone to be able to demonstrate in peace, we
> want to show respect for all the victims and that the
> demonstration should be peaceful,' she said. (Graham-
> Harrison, 10 January 2015)

4.3. Controversy over the Video

As noted above, the video of Merabet's death was the premise of the attention focused on Merabet. The video itself and frames captured from the video gained massive circulation, which then again fuelled attention and public debate. The family were deeply disturbed and upset by the images. Morgane Ahmad told BBC News (10 January 2015)[8] that she had first learned about her partner's death on television, although she hadn't recognized him in the video:

---

[7]https://www.theguardian.com/world/2015/jan/10/charlie-hebdo-policeman-murder-ahmed-merabet (Retrieved 10 October 2017).
[8]http://www.bbc.com/news/world-europe-30761229 (Retrieved 10 October 2017).

> I was in a restaurant and a television was on [...] I didn't recognise him, I only saw the picture of a man on the pavement. I tried to call him, sent messages. I went back to work, and then his sister called me.

In the meantime, Jordi Mir was also attracting publicity for filming the shooting and sharing the footage. Mir gave interviews in which he apologized to the family and to the general public for sharing his video on social media. In the words of a headline by *Time* on 11 January 2015,[9] 'Man Who Filmed Terrorists Shooting Paris Cop Says He Regrets Sharing Video.' In the original interview by the Associated Press,[10] Jordi Mir describes his actions as a 'stupid reflex':

> 'I was completely panicked,' he said in an exclusive interview across from the Parisian boulevard where the officer was shot to death by terrorists Wednesday morning. [...] 'I had to speak to someone,' Mir said. 'I was alone in my flat. I put the video on Facebook. That was my error.'

Later in the same interview, he reflects on his decision to publish the video as part of the wider social media culture:

> 'There's no answer,' he said. Perhaps a decade of social networking had trained him to share whatever he saw. [...] 'I take a photo — a cat — and I put it on Facebook. It was the same stupid reflex,' he said. ... 'On Facebook, there's no confidentiality,' he said. 'It's a lesson for me.'

Jordi Mir also publicly apologized to Merabet's family for posting the video. Prime Minister Manuel Valls joined Merabet's relatives in condemning in the strongest terms the media that published screenshots of Merabet's body. Although reactions to the publication of Mir's video and screenshots varied, they mostly acknowledged the value of the material as visual evidence of the attacks.

The discussion on the video and images of the shooting and the body of Merabet highlights the question of attention in a hybrid media event.

---

[9]http://time.com/3662914/paris-attack-video/ (Retrieved 10 October 2017).
[10]https://www.apnews.com/5e1ee93021b941629186882f03f1bb79 (Retrieved 10 October 2017).

Using the material as criminal evidence of the attack would not have required public circulation. The question of what is and what needs to be published or available for public circulation is one of the issues that has become blurred — perhaps hybridized — as the decision on what gets to be circulated is no longer in the hands of professional news journalists. These issues also feature prominently in Chapter 6, where we discuss the acceleration of circulation in hybrid media events.

4.4.   'Je Suis Ahmed' as a Symbol of Public Solidarity

Ahmed Merabet's family were drawn to the centre of attention unwillingly, and they were very critical of the public circulation of pictures of their family member's death. However, they became the public face of mourning and personalized the sense of loss felt by the general public, including Muslims. The press reported on a particularly touching press conference by Malek in which he spoke against Islamophobia and anti-semitism and condemned the attacks:

> Islam is a religion of peace, love and sharing. It's not about terrorism, it's not about madness — we have nothing to do with that ... My brother was a Muslim and he was killed by people pretending to be Muslims. They are terrorists — that's it. ... I speak now to all the racists, Islamophobes and anti-Semites who confuse extremists and Muslims. Madness has neither colour nor religion. (Alexander, 11 January 2015)[11]

Merabet's family made these comments in an attempt to counter the main narrative that portrayed Muslims as terrorists. They were communicating the sentiments of the Muslim community who were equally horrified by the massacre and who felt insulted by the connection made by the perpetrators between the killings and Islam. Merabet's family were conveying a message of peace, calm and unity, a viewpoint that received much attention and appreciation in the news media.

Ahmed Merabet and his family also received huge outpourings of public sympathy in both the news and social media. Different versions of

---

[11]http://www.telegraph.co.uk/news/worldnews/europe/france/11338404/Funeral-for-French-policeman-Ahmed-Merabet-held-in-Paris.html (Retrieved 18 July 2016).

the slogan, hashtag and message 'Je suis Ahmed' were widely circulated on different platforms. As discussed earlier in Chapter 3, one tweet in particular grasped much attention. It said: 'I am not Charlie, I am Ahmed the dead cop. Charlie ridiculed my faith and culture and I died defending his right to do so' #JesuisAhmed. It became one of the most retweeted messages in the aftermath of the attacks and signalled explicit solidarity for Merabet and what he represented as a Muslim and French citizen. The *Daily Mail* (Bentley, 8 January 2015; Mullin & Boyle, 2015)[12] had this headline: '"He Died Defending the Right to Ridicule His Faith": France Unites behind #JeSuisAhmed on Twitter in Tribute to Muslim Officer Slain by Fanatics as He Begged for His Life.' The story described how thousands of people had paid tribute to the dead Muslim police officer using the rallying cry 'Je suis Ahmed'. These activities were interpreted as expressions of admiration for Merabet's sacrifice while defending the right to freedom of speech. The story also reproduced some tweets to demonstrate those performances of solidarity. *The New York Times* (Breed, 8 January 2015)[13] interpreted those expressions of solidarity around 'Je suis Ahmed' by saying that 'users praised him as a hero and, in some cases, a potent symbol in the debate about free speech and religious tolerance'.

Another key element in these demonstrations of symbolic solidarity for Merabet was a photo in which he was smiling directly at the camera, with a sense of joy and optimism. This image was used in connection with the news about Ahmed Merabet's death and the ensuing public mourning, and in connection with messages of solidarity circulating in social media. In addition, a spontaneous memorial site overflowing with flowers, candles and pictures was created on the side of a pavement in the neighbourhood where Merabet had lived.

Merabet's funeral also attracted much attention in the news and social media. The highly mediatized funeral consisted of two parts, an official homage in the city centre (a ceremony in remembrance of the three police officers killed in the attacks) and the Muslim burial in Bobigny. *The Guardian*'s (Willsher, 13 January 2015)[14] funeral report

---

[12]http://www.dailymail.co.uk/news/article-2901681/Hero-police-officer-executed-street-married-42-year-old-Muslim-assigned-patrol-Paris-neighbourhood-Charlie-Hebdo-offices-located.html (Retrieved 10 October 2017).
[13]https://www.nytimes.com/2015/01/09/world/europe/charlie-hebdo-terror-attack-je-suis-ahmed-merabet.html (Retrieved 10 October 2017).
[14]https://www.theguardian.com/world/2015/jan/13/charlie-hebdo-attack-ahmed-merabet-buried-bobigny (Retrieved 23 September 2017).

described the emotional attachment to Merabet's life and death at the office as heroic and patriotic:

> His Tricolor-draped coffin arrived to a crowd of silent mourners. On the flag were his képi and the Légion d'Honneur placed there earlier by the French president, François Hollande, who described Merabet as a symbol of the 'diversity of France's forces of law and order'.
>
> 'He was very proud to represent the French republic,' Hollande said after posthumously awarding the three officers killed in last week's attacks in Paris the highest honour in France.
>
> 'Ahmed Merabet knew better than anyone that radical Islam has nothing to do with Islam and that fanaticism kills Muslims,' the president said.

In a report on the funeral guests' reactions, *Al Jazeera English* (14 January 2015)[15] described how Merabet's friends and Muslim religious leaders spoke of Merabet as an officer who managed to reconcile his dual identity as a French citizen and a Muslim. News coverage in general was respectful, describing Merabet as 'a genuine good cop' (AFP, 13 January 2015)[16] whose life had set an example for the Muslim community and whose death was a loss, not only for his family and loved ones, but society at large. The message of brotherhood and unity is repeated by leaders of the French Muslim and Jewish community, friends and colleagues in a YouTube video by AFP news agency (13 January 2015)[17] on Merabet's funeral ceremony.

In the coverage of the funeral, Merabet's Muslim body came to symbolize harmony, the idea that it was possible to live in peace and serve French society as a Muslim (cf. Butler, 2004). This message of an 'ideal Muslim' as synonymous with an 'ideal victim' (cf. Greer, 2004) was central to Hollande's public speech after Merabet's death, and it was also highlighted in the public addresses by his brother.

---

[15] http://www.aljazeera.com/video/europe/2015/01/tribute-paid-slain-french-muslim-policeman-2015113215020146152.html (Retrieved 23 September 2017).
[16] https://www.youtube.com/watch?v=26VgrG1nOvk (Retrieved 23 September 2017).
[17] https://www.youtube.com/watch?v=26VgrG1nOvk (Retrieved 19 July 2017).

4.5.   Politicizing the Muslim Body

The inclination towards unity, or what some commentators have described as 'the Charlie Effect' (see, e.g., Titley, 2017), had immediate political implications and was used in different ways for different political purposes.

The French political establishment, most notably President Hollande and Prime Minister Manuel Valls, praised Merabet as an exemplary Muslim and French citizen. In an official ceremony, Merabet and two other police officers were awarded the Légion d'Honneur, the highest order of recognition in France. As well as giving public speeches in which they highlighted Merabet's exemplary role, Hollande and Valls took active part in the public mourning of Merabet. Hollande also paid a visit to Merabet's family in Seine-Saint-Denis, a symbolic act that also received attention in the media (e.g., *Le Parisien*, 11 January 2015).[18] It was reported that Valls was visibly emotionally moved in the ceremony (BFMTV, 13 January 2015).[19]

Viewed from another angle, the rhetoric of the ruling elite was less conciliatory. Prime Minister Manuel Valls, for example, declared war on radical Islam, stating in *New York Times*: 'It is a war against terrorism, against jihadism, against radical Islam, against everything that is aimed at breaking fraternity, freedom, solidarity' (Bilefsky & de la Baume, 10 January 2015).[20] This comment, quickly associated with the rhetoric of US President George W. Bush after the 9/11 attacks, attracted considerable interest in the international news media (see, e.g., Goyette, 10 January 2015[21]; *Financial Times*, 13 January 2015[22]; BBC News, 13 January 2015[23]).

President Hollande, too, called for action against terrorism (De Royer, 10 January 2015).[24] At the other end of the political spectrum,

---

[18] http://www.leparisien.fr/livry-gargan-93190/francois-hollande-rend-visite-a-la-famille-du-policier-ahmed-merabet-11-01-2015-4437653.php (Retrieved 17 October 2017).
[19] http://www.bfmtv.com/politique/hommage-aux-policiers-tues-les-larmes-retenues-de-manuel-valls-857129.html (Retrieved 17 October 2017).
[20] https://www.nytimes.com/2015/01/11/world/europe/paris-terrorist-attacks.html (Retrieved 12 October 2017).
[21] https://www.huffingtonpost.com/2015/01/10/manuel-valls-radical-islam_n_6449414.html (Retrieved 17 October 2017).
[22] https://www.ft.com/content/49760ad6-9b47-11e4-950f-00144feabdc0 (Retrieved 17 October 2017).
[23] http://www.bbc.com/news/world-europe-30794973 (Retrieved 17 October 2017).
[24] http://www.lefigaro.fr/politique/2015/01/09/01002-20150109ARTFIG00331-dans-la-crise-hollande-se-veut-le-garant-de-l-unite.php (Retrieved 17 October 2017).

right-wing populist leader Marine Le Pen spoke out passionately against 'fundamentalism' in the immediate aftermath of the attacks. According to *The Daily Telegraph* (Watt, 7 January 2015),[25] she called it a 'murderous ideology' and criticized the French political elite for its 'hypocrisy' on the Islam issue:

> 'It is my responsibility to make sure that the fear is overcome,' she said. 'This attack must instead free our speech about Islamic fundamentalism. We must not be silenced.'

In one of her public addresses, Le Pen called for the reinstatement of the death penalty. Her extreme reactions received significant attention in the French and international news media. *The Independent*[26] (Saul, 8 January 2015), among others, voiced concern about the rise of anti-Islam sentiment, Islamophobia and xenophobia following the attacks in French and Western political life.

All in all, the French political debate and the media attention in the aftermath of the *Charlie Hebdo* attacks were very much focused on Islam. The body of Ahmed Merabet became a central symbol in this debate. By expressing solidarity with Merabet and his fate and by saying 'Je suis Ahmed', President Hollande, Prime Minister Valls and the rest of the political leadership in the country wanted to send a public message of unity, of which Merabet's body served as an iconic example. However, this unity was highly conditional, and only included those who were willing and able to accept the principles of the French Republic, namely laïcité and free speech, and to assimilate their ethnic and religious identities with this major principle (see also Titley, 2017).

4.6. Accumulation and Circulation of Attention

The hybridization of the *Charlie Hebdo* media event is empirically demonstrated in the circulation and accumulation of attention in the killing of Ahmed Merabet, and particularly in the question of publicity

---

[25]http://www.telegraph.co.uk/news/11331595/Marine-Le-Pen-condemns-murderous-ideology-in-the-aftermath-of-Charlie-Hebdo-shooting.html (Retrieved 12 October 2017).
[26]http://www.independent.co.uk/news/world/europe/charlie-hebdo-shooting-far-right-front-national-leader-marine-le-pen-wants-to-offer-france-9965607.html (Retrieved 31 October 2017).

discussed above. In other words, it is reflected in the hybridized relationship between social media and mainstream media and in the blurring of boundaries between users and producers. The video of the killing was posted on social media (Facebook) by one private citizen, and circulated to YouTube by another. There was no gatekeeping in either instance. The video and still images from the video were then taken up by professional media, which continued to circulate the material and so spread it to even more social media users. Had it not been for the publishing possibilities provided by social media, the video — had it been recorded in the first place — would probably only have been used by the police as evidence.

It is safe to say that without the video, the shooting of Ahmed Merabet would have gained significantly less attention, for the simple reason that there would have been no discussion about the video and ethical concerns surrounding the video. In a hybrid media event, then, there are always unpredictable elements in the circulation of meanings and the directions that the attention takes. The direction of attention is dependent on the footage available, on power relations and on the affectiveness of the footage. Something that doesn't exist cannot circulate, but when it does exist the circulation of a video or an image strengthens the cultural, symbolic and narrative weight of an event.

In the public attention surrounding Ahmed Merabet's shooting, the statements issued by family members and politicians were part of a narrative that on the one hand challenged the hegemonic narrative and metonymic connection (Ahmed 2004a, 2004b) between Islam and terrorism, and its embodiment in the Muslim body. On the other hand, the 'us' in whose ranks Merabet was included was quite limited and exclusive. On the other hand, these statements assigned Merabet to the ranks of a rather limited and exclusive 'us'.

Since the video did exist, and since Ahmed Merabet's relatives were willing to take part in the public discussion, Merabet became an 'ideal victim' (Greer, 2004). He gained the attention of politicians and news media as a 'good Muslim', as an assimilated and secularized part of the Western 'us', French society. At the same time, the vast majority of the political discussion focused on strengthening the connection between Islam — or the male Muslim body — and terrorism. This affective stickiness is discussed further in the next chapter.

Chapter 5

Affect

Terror attacks are in large part intended to elicit responses of affect: anxiety, fear, horror and disgust (see, e.g., Kepel, 2017; Roy, 2016). The highly mediatized and global media events following the *Charlie Hebdo* attacks certainly achieved that goal. The response in the news and social media was highly affective, although the tone and style did vary widely. In the news coverage, mainstream media sought to strike a balance between, what Risto Kunelius and Hillel Nossek (2008) have called 'the rational and the ritual' in disruptive media events, between subject-centred dispassionate reporting and emotionally laden testimonies. In social media, emotions of empathy and solidarity with the *Charlie Hebdo* victims were expressed more openly.

But there were also emotional reactions of a different kind to the *Charlie Hebdo* attacks and their aftermath. In this chapter, we are interested as well in those reactions that challenged the prominent 'Je suis Charlie' responses. Many of these counter-emotional social media reactions denounced *Charlie Hebdo* and the newspaper's supporters as grossly offensive and Islamophobic (see, e.g., Dawes, 2017). In his introduction to *After Charlie Hebdo: Terror, Racism and Free Speech*, Gavan Titley (2017, pp. 1–2) describes the emotional atmosphere immediately after the killings: 'A dense field of meaning-making and affect took shape around *Charlie Hebdo*, and positioned it as a mediating object for a knot of political tensions, competing imaginaries and interpretative conflicts that have been taking shape and gathering force in European public spheres for several decades.'

In this chapter, we start from Sara Ahmed's (2004a, 2004b) idea of affects and emotions as 'sticky', as social and cultural practices that through circulation accumulate and associate with certain actors, bodies and signs. We argue that in a violent hybrid media event, circulating affects play a crucial role in gaining and accumulating attention and in managing narrative meanings and symbolic and ideological battles associated with the event. A violent terrorist occurrence, such as the *Charlie Hebdo* attacks, can generate a collective, 'public outpouring of emotion' (Marlière, 2017), which is amplified through the mediatized communication and affordances provided by the hybrid media environment. Through the circulation of representations — memes, texts, videos, tweets — solidarity and hate are connected with particular cultural and bodily signifiers, establishing sticky connections between, in this instance, dark skin, Muslim and terrorism.

One significant social and cultural practice in stirring and managing emotions in media events is that of ritual. In Dayan and Katz's (1992) original media event theory, ritual refers to the ceremonial aspects of media events and their highly symbolic, scripted and patterned character. Later, Katz and Liebes (2007) argued that in disruptive media events caused by unexpected violence, ritual aspects can also be identified in the perpetrators' activities (e.g. highly scripted terror attacks) and in the public's ritual responses (Sumiala, 2013). These include a wide range of media-related practices, such as gathering in public spaces with placards and symbols and creating memorial sites and spontaneous shrines; posting and sharing images of these activities on digital media platforms; tweeting ritualized messages; changing profile pictures to pay tribute to the victims and making and circulating memes and videos of mourning (cf. Sumiala, 2013).

In this line of thinking, digital rituals share many features in common with the rituals that were performed in 'offline' contexts. Both online and offline rituals involve elements of symbolic communication, require participant involvement, are carried out in certain times and spaces and, when successful, have an impact on the lives of the participants (see, e.g., Sumiala, 2013). The digital ritual typically appears in a very particular context, which causes us to expand our conceptions of affect into something more fluid, mobile, multi-temporal, multi-sited and, hence, rather heterogeneous (Sumiala, 2014). This multiplication of the dimensions of ritual in digital media also engenders a polyphony of interpretations regarding what is happening and what it signifies. Not all voices have the same power, but the potential for contradictory interpretations of this ritual act of granting the deceased a new identity makes the rite unpredictable and difficult to control. In analysing the circulation of emotions in those ritual practices, we must also pay attention to how certain ritual practices (of solidarity) frame and legitimize emotional responses and by the same token marginalize and delegitimize other emotional responses and their ritual practices (see also Dawes, 2017, p. 183).

Next, we examine in detail the mediatized ritualization that evolved as an emotional response to the *Charlie Hebdo* attacks. We begin by providing a thick description of the ritual activities created around

'Je suis Charlie' and then move on to describe some counter-ritual and emotional activities that were stirred up by the sense of resentment, anger and frustration towards what was portrayed as emotional unity. In this analysis of the circulation of emotions attached to ritual practices, we give special focus to the hybrid dynamics between professional and ordinary media users and their respective platforms, to the multi-layered dynamics between physical and virtual activities in offline and online contexts and to the symbolic and ideological battles between those collective activities and related identities.

5.1.   Rituals Intensify the Sense of Solidarity in Media

Not surprisingly, Paris became the ritual heart of the public expressions of solidarity following the *Charlie Hebdo* attacks. Both the news and social media began to circulate images of people gathering in demonstrations on the streets and in the squares of Paris on the very first evening after the attacks. People came together to show solidarity with the victims by carrying 'Je suis Charlie' pens and placards. Candles were lit and people spontaneously chanted together. In those rituals, emotions of sadness and grief were embedded in broader symbolic and ideological frameworks, such as taking a stand against violence and defending the values of the French Republic, particularly freedom of expression and speech as well as the principle of laïcité (see also Titley, 2017).

The Place de la République and the statue of Marianne, a defining symbol of the French Revolution, assumed special visual significance in the media. Joachim Roncin, creator of the 'Je suis Charlie' meme, later explained in a BBC interview (3 January 2016)[1] what the slogan was intended to capture: 'We're trying to feel a community … It is very reassuring to be all together whenever there is something horrible happening.' In a CNN YouTube news video clip (7 January 2015),[2] for example, people are gathered in the square and holding 'Je suis Charlie' placards and pens. This visual image is accompanied by emotional background music. The title of the video reads, 'Je suis Charlie. Paris gathers after terror attack.' The clip has quite a respectful tone. *Le Monde*, *Libération* and *The New York Times*, to name just a few, also posted videos on their websites to demonstrate the public mourning

---

[1]http://www.bbc.com/news/blogs-trending-35108339 (Retrieved 7 February 2017).
[2]https://www.youtube.com/watch?v=vWkdmLH7xdE (Retrieved 23 September 2017).

after the attacks in Paris. *The Guardian* (Willsher & Quinn, 7 January 2015)[3] describes the emotional atmosphere in Paris as follows:

> As night fell, Parisians gathered under the imposing statue of Marianne, her extended right arm holding an olive branch, the symbol of peace.
>
> They gathered in shock to show their anger, grief and solidarity.
>
> Some lit candles that were arranged to spell out the words Je Suis Charlie, the new slogan of support and condolence for those who died at the offices of *Charlie Hebdo*.
>
> Others held up hastily made banners or copies of the magazine's front pages past and current, including one of a Muslim kissing Charb, the cartoonist and editor, under the headline: 'Love is stronger than hate'.
>
> Some held up pens; a simple but powerful gesture of support for the journalists gunned down just hours before.

Those interviewed by the paper explained their motives to join the demonstrations as follows:

> 'We need to show the terrorists that they cannot win', said Jules, a student.
>
> 'Everyone is shocked: the cartoonists Charb, Cabu, Wolinski, Tikgnous [...] we grew up with them. Half of France grew up with them', said one man, who did not want to be named, who was, like many in the crowd, close to tears.
>
> [...] Friends greeted each other with hugs. Strangers with a grim nod of the head and a frown. There was a sense of collective comfort even for those who came alone.

French and Western news media played a central part in elevating the ritual practices around the slogan 'Je suis Charlie', a symbol of

---

[3]https://www.theguardian.com/world/2015/jan/07/rallies-charlie-hebdo-paris-london-solidarity-grief (Retrieved 1 October 2017).

(trans)national unity. Countless reports on public expressions of solidarity not only in Paris, France, but also around the world and the internet, communicated a sense of unanimous unity.

As Dawes (2017) points out, it took several days, at least for the French news media, to acknowledge the polyphony of emotional responses. Counter-emotional responses first began to emerge in the social media through such slogans and hashtags as #JeNeSuisPasCharlie ('I am not Charlie'). In many cases, the message was not to support the killings, but to take issue with what was considered as an excessive display of solidarity with questionable symbolic and ideological manifestations of racism and Islamophobia (Badouard, 2016; Dawes, 2017). We revert to these counter-emotional responses towards the end of this chapter.

Other ritual practices also developed within the most prominent emotional frame of solidarity. One was that of a ritual pilgrimage (see, e.g., Coleman & Elsner, 1998; Eade & Sallinow, 1999), offline and online journeys to places of high symbolic value. One spontaneous shrine, the street outside the *Charlie Hebdo* offices, turned into a sea of flowers and notes of condolences. Images of people descending upon this site of mourning were circulated in the news media and on social networking sites. This pilgrimage also involved people taking selfies at the site, thus creating an offline−online connection in the ritualized public mourning.

Offline and online pilgrimages were also made to the Eiffel Tower. The lights of the tower were switched off on 8 January, a ritual gesture that received massive attention in the media. The *Daily Mail* (Bentley, 8 January 2015; Mullin & Boyle, 2015)[4] headline read: 'Paris goes dark for *Charlie Hebdo*: Eiffel Tower's lights are turned off as vigils are held around globe for 12 victims slaughtered by fanatics.' National tributes were paid at the Place des Terreaux in Lyon, in the centre of Marseille and numerous other locations of intensified symbolic relevance and meaning.

In the news media, the waves of public solidarity extended far beyond the borders of France, across Europe and around the world. In London, people gathered together on several occasions to pay tribute to the victims of *Charlie Hebdo* and performed public rituals of solidarity by creating circles of pens in Trafalgar Square. One demonstrator

---

[4]http://www.dailymail.co.uk/news/article-2902025/France-comes-standstill-remember-Charlie-Hebdo-victims-people-worldwide-join-poignant-vigil.html   (Retrieved 7 January 2017).

holding a 'Je suis Charlie' placard and a brush in her hand said in tears: 'Today I am full of anger, and tomorrow I will be very, very sad' (Walt, 8 January 2015).[5] In Berlin, people gathered at the Brandenburg Gate to pay tributes and express solidarity. In Moscow, people brought flowers, candles and notes of condolence to the French embassy. French embassies served as spatial representations of France in mourning in many other cities as well. As reported among others by *Time*,[6] *Libération* (2015)[7] and *Le Monde*,[8] *Charlie Hebdo* vigils were held in cities around the world, including Melbourne, Montreal, Madrid, Washington DC, New York City, Istanbul and Rio de Janeiro. The message of these gatherings was to defend freedom of expression, hence the slogan 'Je suis Charlie'.

Yet another, highly mediatized ritual performance of solidarity was carried out on 11 January 2015 when some 40 world leaders, including German Chancellor Angela Merkel, British Prime Minister David Cameron and French President François Hollande joined millions of people who staged public demonstrations (which became known as republican marches) on the streets of Paris and elsewhere in France. The public spectacle made massive headlines around the world and prompted much activity on social networking sites. *The New York Times* (Alderman & Bilefsky, 11 January 2015)[9] wrote: 'Huge Show of Solidarity in Paris against Terrorism', while *The Independent* (Lichfield, 11 January 2015)[10] led its coverage with the headline, 'Paris March: Global Leaders Join "Unprecedented" Rally in Largest Demonstration in History of France.' The emotional tone of much of the Western news coverage was supportive and sympathetic to the demonstration, although the involvement of Israeli Prime Minister Benjamin Netanyahu and Palestinian Authority President Mahmoud Abbas also gave rise to some political controversy and critical commentary. President Barak Obama's

---

[5]http://time.com/3659164/charlie-hebdo-paris-suspects/ (Retrieved 23 September 2017).
[6]http://time.com/3660809/charlie-hebdo-paris-reactions/ (Retrieved 23 September 2017).
[7]http://www.liberation.fr/video/2015/01/08/charlie-hebdo-un-hommage-mondial_1176339 (Retrieved 23 September 2017).
[8]http://www.lemonde.fr/attaque-contre-charlie-hebdo/video/2015/01/08/hommage-mondial-pour-charlie-hebdo_4551263_4550668.html (Retrieved 23 September 2017).
[9]https://www.nytimes.com/2015/01/12/world/europe/paris-march-against-terror-charlie-hebdo.html (Retrieved 5 February 2017).
[10]http://www.independent.co.uk/news/world/europe/world-leaders-gather-for-freedom-march-in-paris-as-million-expected-at-rally-9970512.html (Retrieved 7 February 2017).

absence from the Paris march also raised some eyebrows (see, e.g., *The Telegraph*, 12 January 2015).[11] Both at the physical sites of these demonstrations and on media platforms, all these ritual practices of solidarity and visits to sites of special significance were characterized by a complex interplay between offline and online ritualizations. The sense of global public solidarity was first and foremost constructed and communicated not only by the news media but also and importantly by social media. This sense profoundly shaped the prominent narrative of the media event as a spectacle of (trans)national unity.

5.2. 'Je Suis Charlie' in Social Media

Ordinary people of different nationalities created and posted large numbers of YouTube videos to pay tribute to and commemorate the victims. Many of these videos included rich symbolic visualizations expressing solidarity with the victims. One of them, created by username Eloïse Derquenne[12] is titled 'Je suis *Charlie Hebdo* Hommage/Tribute'. Downloaded on 8 January 2015, just one day after the attacks, the video includes music, still and live images and messages expressing solidarity and defending the values of freedom of expression. Another YouTube video by username Striks Vindicta[13] has the title 'Vidéo de l'Hommage Mondiale à *Charlie Hebdo*'. It also includes music and images of people gathering together around the world to mourn the victims of the *Charlie Hebdo* attacks. The slogan 'Je suis Charlie' is repeated over and over in the images. There were also artistic interventions on various platforms and online sites. Professional and amateur artists contributed to the ritualization of the event by drawing cartoons and making and remaking other visual and political commentaries, such as songs composed, recorded and posted on YouTube, and Facebook feeds covered by messages of 'Je suis Charlie'.[14]

On Twitter, ritual practices involved circulating photos of solidarity demonstrations and tributes in different cities. One of the most shared

---

[11]http://www.telegraph.co.uk/news/worldnews/europe/france/11339477/US-media-questions-why-neither-Barack-Obama-nor-top-US-officials-attended-Paris-Charlie-Hebdo-rally.html (Retrieved 23 September 2017).
[12]https://www.youtube.com/watch?v=4gpsYWYkq6U (Retrieved 5 February 2017).
[13]https://www.youtube.com/watch?v=TNMPxqCVFlc (Retrieved 5 February 2017).
[14]See, e.g., https://www.youtube.com/watch?v=-bjbUg9d64g (Retrieved 5 February 2017).

photos on Twitter was an aerial shot from Lyon, taken on the evening of 7 January and showing a crowd gathered around the steps at the Place des Terreaux. The steps were covered with hundreds of lit candles, a glowing shrine in the darkness. Other prominent images portrayed people carrying 'We are not afraid' signs and holding up pens in memory of the cartoonists. These photos were accompanied by messages of defiance and unity, such as 'This is how you encounter terrorism. #JeSuisCharlie' and 'Paris, tonight. We stand with you, from all over the world. Not afraid. #JeSuisCharlie'.

5.3. Funerals

In addition to the offline and online public rituals of solidarity, some of the victims' funerals gained ritual significance in the news media and on social networking sites, and were thus used to underline the sense of unity and solidarity stirred up by the attacks. The funerals on 15 January 2015 reported in the news media included elements of traditional, ceremonial media events (see, e.g., Samuel, 15 January 2015).[15]

In many of the news clips and YouTube videos on the funerals, emotional messages of solidarity were communicated to the audience not only through interviews with family members, but also by giving voice to the members of the public who came to take part in the funeral rite. Many of those comments by the public expressed solidarity with the victims and the values advocated by the cartoonists. Some participants said they had decided to attend the funeral specifically to express their support for those values. In a report by *Daily Mirror*[16] on 15 January, daughter of the murdered cartoonist Georges Wolinski, Elsa Wolinski expressed her thoughts and feelings as follows:

> I'm beginning to realise that he is gone. But as I said before, they've killed a man and not his ideas.
>
> So here we are. We stand here and we will continue to defend the principles of *Charlie Hebdo*.

---

[15]http://www.telegraph.co.uk/news/worldnews/europe/france/11348620/Charlie-Hebdo-cartoonist-funerals-held-in-Paris-as-million-more-copies-sell-out.html   (Retrieved   23 September 2017).
[16]http://www.mirror.co.uk/news/world-news/charlie-hebdo-funerals-guardian-angel-4987381 (Retrieved 23 September 2017).

Among the other victims, the funeral of police officer Ahmed Merabet received special public attention. As discussed in Chapter 4, Merabet's was the only death that was filmed and recorded, and then put into circulation in the digital media. Consequently, it received massive public visibility and became a subject of public mourning under the slogan 'Je suis Ahmed'. Merabet's funeral became mediatized and consisted of two parts, the official homage in the city centre (a ceremony in remembrance of the three police officers killed in the attacks) and the Muslim burial in Bobigny.

News coverage of the funerals of the four Jewish victims at the kosher supermarket in Paris also addressed the public mourning and the presence and participation of state leaders, namely Israeli Prime Minister Benjamin Netanyahu and President Reuven Rivlin, French Environment Minister Ségolène Royal and religious leaders such as Chief Rabbi for Jerusalem Avraham Stern. All the victims were French Jews, but their bodies had been flown to Jerusalem to be buried. *The Telegraph* (Line, 13 January 2015)[17] describes the atmosphere at the funeral:

> Volunteers carried the bodies of the victims, wrapped in Israel flags, to the cemetery [...]
>
> Crowds lined the streets of Jerusalem to pay their respects, many with signs stating: 'Je suis Juif' and 'Je suis Israelien' above photographs of the victims.
>
> Another man held a sign which read: 'I am dead because I'm Jewish', above a photograph of the victims.
>
> Relatives of the victims each spoke briefly and lit a torch in memory of their loved one.
>
> The Chief Rabbi for Jerusalem, Avraham Stern, used scissors to cut the shirts of the relatives — a traditional Jewish sign of mourning.

The reactions and responses of the politicians participating in the funeral are described in the following manner:

---

[17]http://www.telegraph.co.uk/news/worldnews/middleeast/israel/11342184/Jewish-victims-of-Paris-shootings-mourned-at-Israeli-funeral.html (Retrieved 23 September 2017).

Prime Minister Benjamin Netanyahu said: 'Four dear people, honest and full of love, like the victims from Toulouse who are buried here, were killed solely for being Jews. Their lives were cut short in an attack of hatred by a lowly murderer'.

'I have been saying for many years and I say it again today: These are not only enemies of the Jewish people; they are enemies of all mankind. It is time all people of culture to unite and uproot these enemies from our midst'.

The ritual public expression of solidarity following the *Charlie Hebdo* attacks took place on a variety of digital media platforms, and it was conducted by both professional and ordinary media users. It involved multiple modes of media-related and media-saturated symbolic communication (rituals of grief, rituals of paying tribute, funerary rituals). However, this multiplication of digital ritual practices should not be interpreted only in terms of a quantified representation of solidarity. It also revealed a hierarchy between the victims and their social and cultural significance. Among the police officers killed, the death of Ahmed Merabet received much more exposure than the killings of his two colleagues. Merabet's death and the public mourning that followed served a definite purpose in the narrative construction of the event: Merabet was a mediating Muslim body between the victims and the radical perpetrators. This narrative was constantly repeated in the official French response, notably in President Hollande's public appearances: his addresses at memorial services, visits to certain sites and official attendance at Merabet's funeral service. The cartoonists' funerals (some of which were held in private) also became ceremonial media events that highlighted, both in words and in images, the role of cartoonists in the defence of Western freedom. In the case of the Jewish victims, the symbolic act of flying their bodies to the 'promised land' served to link their deaths with those of previous generations killed by antisemitic violence.

Whatever the motives behind the mediatization and circulation of these funerals on various media platforms, the quantified multimedia representation of public mourning contributed to the social construction of the emotional experience of these incidents in this hybrid media event as a celebration of solidarity and unity. In both the news and social media, the emotional prominence given to the *Charlie Hebdo* attacks served as an expression of sympathy and solidarity with the victims. These emotional responses through the medium of highly ritualized practices were deeply embedded in the symbolic and ideological battles waged over the meaning of the attacks and their social, political and cultural implications in 'Western societies', particularly in France. Gavan Titley (2017, p. 2) has the following critical assessment of the nature of these battles:

> It explores the ways in which the attacks in Paris in 2015 acquired such accelerated and (unevenly) globalised symbolic weight, and examines their political and cultural generativity in France, and elsewhere, in terms of five key themes: the drive to use '*Charlie Hebdo*' as a catalyst for renewing the French Republic, particularly through the remit of the nationalist state secularism of laïcité; the prolonged, shape-shifting 'war on terror' and the impact of securitarian and culturalist responses to attacks; the politics of freedom of expression in a context of abundant communication; the political generativity of accelerated and instantaneous networked media coverage; and the challenges for anti-racist thought and activism in the context of 'post-racial' politics.

In the last part of this chapter, we turn our attention to the emotional responses that criticized the hegemony of the 'Je suis Charlie' narrative as a prominent frame of interpretation of the event.

5.4. Narratives Opposed to 'Je Suis Charlie' Solidarity

The *Charlie Hebdo* attacks did not elicit just one unanimous emotional response or ritual reaction. The responses articulated and ritualized in the media also included expressions of resentment, hate, anger and frustration. As discussed earlier, one of the hashtags circulating in the media was 'Je ne suis pas Charlie' ('I am not Charlie'). We maintain that the purpose of this hashtag was to argue that the unanimous show of solidarity in response to the attacks was little more than a façade. In his article on the formation of an ad hoc public around the hashtags #JeSuisCharlie and #JeNeSuisPasCharlie, Dawes (2017, pp. 188–189) has the following explanation for the hashtag 'Je ne suis pas Charlie:'

> The members of the #JeNeSuisPasCharlie hashtag community did not speak with one voice or one call for action. Rather, participants in the conversation sought

to express and formulate their shared reaction to the dominant frame. Some spoke as Muslims, others on behalf of Muslims, and others distanced themselves from the magazine for reasons that had nothing to do with communitarianism, let alone a rejection of Republican values. The hashtag was not about support for terrorism or collective action; rather, its primary goal was for users to form, enhance and declare their self-identity, with the hashtag serving as a vehicle through which a collective identity could be developed by distinction. (Giglietto & Lee, 2015)

In this frame of thinking, 'Je ne suis pas Charlie' should be understood as an emotional expression of a willingness to participate in a much larger conversation that contributes to making sense of the attacks and their cultural, political and social implications (see also Dawes, 2017, p. 194).

Other emotional responses also emerged in the news and social media. Protests were reported in different parts of the (Muslim) world, including countries such as Pakistan, Afghanistan, Yemen and Nigeria. Protests were also seen in London and other multicultural and multireligious world cities (see, e.g., *The Guardian*, 8 February 2015).[18] Slogans such as 'Je suis musulman' ('I am Muslim'), but also 'Je suis musulman, pas terroriste' ('I am Muslim, not terrorist') appeared as symbols of ritual resistance in the digital media. Furthermore, many YouTube videos communicated a message of anger against *Charlie Hebdo* and its presumed Islamophobia. The pictures published by *Charlie Hebdo* of the Prophet Muhammad were considered disrespectful towards the sacred values of Muslims, and hence to cause offence to Islam and its principles (cf. Brown, 2009). While it would be misleading to describe these ritualized performances as carnevalizing death, they certainly were a counter-narrative performance against the public articulation of solidarity for the victims of the *Charlie Hebdo* attacks (see, e.g., *Al Jazeera English*, 19 January 2015).[19]

---

[18]https://www.theguardian.com/world/2015/feb/08/british-muslims-london-protest-against-muhammad-cartoon-charlie-hebdo (Retrieved 5 February 2017).
[19]http://www.aljazeera.com/news/europe/2015/01/anti-charlie-hebdo-protest-held-ch echnya-201511910042173574.html (Retrieved 7 February 2017).

The perpetrators' funerals also attracted attention in the news and social media. To give one example, NBC News (13 January 2015)[20] reported on the Kouachi brothers' funeral in Pakistan, which was held in the absence of bodies:

> A Pakistani cleric has held funerals for Chérif and Saïd Kouachi, the Islamist terrorist brothers behind the *Charlie Hebdo* magazine massacre.
>
> 'Today we feel so proud to attend the funeral of our brothers', said cleric Allama Pir Mohammad Chishti after leading the funeral in absentia in the city of Peshawar. 'They are heroes of Islam. They laid down their lives but eliminated those published caricatures of our Prophet Muhammad'.
>
> [...]
>
> 'We invited all the Muslims to join us as the two brothers had taken stand on our prophet by killing the publisher and cartoonists', said Abdul Aziz, a spokesman of the school that arranged the ceremony held in a public park.
>
> [...]
>
> Mohammad Rasheed Ahmad, a student at the madrassa, said he was disappointed so few came out to honor the Kouachis.
>
> 'We saw tens of thousands of people gathered in France to show solidarity with their slain men, but Muslims didn't come to take part in the funeral of the two heroes who did this great job', he said.

Two days later, *The New York Times* (De la Baume & Bilefsky, 15 January 2015)[21] ran the headline, 'Bodies of French Gunmen Lie Unburied, and, It Appears, Mostly Unwanted,' reporting that the bodies of the three perpetrators — the Kouachi brothers and Coulibaly — remained in the possession of police in Paris and that there had been no

---

[20]https://www.nbcnews.com/storyline/paris-magazine-attack/charlie-hebdo-attack-pakistan-cleric-holds-funerals-kouachi-brothers-n285011 (Retrieved 27 September 2017).
[21]https://www.nytimes.com/2015/01/16/world/europe/bodies-of-french-gunmen-lie-unburied-and-largely-unwanted.html?mcubz=3 (Retrieved 27 September 2017).

indication on behalf of relatives as to how they wanted to bury their dead.

On 23 January, the *International Business Times*[22] carried a story about the secret burials of Coulibaly and the Kouachi brothers in Paris. The reporting is moderate in tone, and references to 'secret funerals' and 'unmarked graves' seem to downplay the funeral ritual and related emotional reactions.

The different emotional registers in which the funerals were covered in the news underscore the complex role of emotions in shaping the sense-making of the event. In some audiences, the funeral reports' celebration of the Kouachi brothers as heroes may have given rise to anxiety, fear and anger, in others these emotions may have helped the audience identify with the killers, their supporters and their assumed goals. The deliberate downplaying of the perpetrators' funerals in France is also significant, and interpreted as an emotional strategy for diminishing the meaning and value of the killers. In a hybrid media event, then, emotional responses must always be thought of in the framework of the attention economy. The greater the visibility given to a phenomenon or actor or incident, of whatever kind, the greater its significance in the narrative of the event. This said, it is important not only to look at what is circulated and what attracts attention in the media, but also to consider those elements and actors that are silenced or ignored in such media events.

5.5. Circulation of Fear Addresses Diverse Audiences

Our examination of the *Charlie Hebdo* attacks in the framework of the circulation of emotions is not complete unless we consider the aspect of fear. Expressions of fear can be identified in many different responses and reactions to the attacks. Condensed in the Muslim body, this fear might stem from concerns not only about potential new attacks against other media professionals and cartoonists criticizing Islam, but also about random attacks against anyone in the street. Fears were also experienced and expressed by different ethnic groups, such as Jews and Muslims. *Al Jazeera America* (Muhammad, 8 January 2015)[23] reported

---

[22]http://www.ibtimes.co.uk/paris-shooting-jihadi-murderer-amedy-coulibaly-given-secret-burial-paris-unmarked-grave-1484857 (Retrieved 27 September 2017).
[23]http://america.aljazeera.com/articles/2015/1/8/in-muslim-neighborhoodsinparisgri efandfear.html (Retrieved 30 September 2017).

on the fear of Islamophobia among the Muslim community in Paris and France:

> [...] Many said the attack, the bloodiest in 50 years in France, will feed an already simmering sentiment against Muslims there. French media reported a number of apparent reprisal incidents directed at Muslim-owned businesses and mosques after the *Charlie Hebdo* shooting.
>
> Rashid Abdulrahim, a 22-year-old finance student, said at first he thought only of the victims and their families when he heard the news of the attack. But when he learned the three suspects were Muslim, he said he immediately felt scared.
>
> 'Things will be really bad for us now. Before the shootings, it was normal for us to be attacked by people who don't like Muslims', he said, 'but now it will be much worse. There will be hate and discrimination and aggression. People will start saying it was right to hate Muslims because they're apparently crazy'.

One ritual response to this fear of terrorism was for people to gather in public places such as the Place de la République in Paris in demonstration against terror. Images of people standing up against the sense of dread and declaring 'we are not afraid' began to circulate in various media.

Importantly enough, this slogan had a historical point of reference to earlier violent attacks in Europe: it was first used after the London underground bombings in 2005 in response to the mass killings (see, e.g., BBC News, 12 July 2005).[24] Since then, campaigns and networks have been created around this slogan to organize opposition against violence and terror in the present age. As a hybrid media event, the circulation of emotions in the *Charlie Hebdo* attacks thus consisted of a wide array of affective responses, even though news stories in Western media in particular were keen to convey a message of unified solidarity. These circulations of emotional responses cut across multiple media platforms and addressed numerous actors horizontally in time and space, but they also relied on schemes of interpretation that already

---

[24]http://news.bbc.co.uk/2/hi/uk_news/england/london/4674425.stm (Retrieved 1 October 2017).

existed in the mnemonic schemes of interpretation of the event, to use the vocabulary of Barbie Zelizer (2018). In addition to the spontaneous emotional responses taking place here and now, and their ritualization in the news and social media, some emotionally laden responses were mainly intended to comment on the massive public wave of solidarity and its inherent embedded injustices.

5.6.   Hybridization and Ritual Practices

Hybrid media events of terrorist violence are highly affective visual spectacles: they very much tap into audiences' emotions as they seek to make sense of the scenes of death and destruction. In order to explore and understand the role of affect as a key dimension of hybrid media events, then, it is imperative to give special focus to the circulation of emotions in such events. As Sara Ahmed (2004a, 2004b) argues, emotions are best thought of as practices on the move, in our case attached to different types of symbolic and material representations and practices of ritual mourning and protest. In this chapter, we have examined the ritual practices of solidarity stirred up by the *Charlie Hebdo* attacks and some counter-narrative and counter-ritual practices challenging those ritual expressions of sympathy for the victims (namely the cartoonists) and the values they represented.

As for exploring hybridity in affect circulation, we must, again, give special focus to the complex dynamics activated between different platforms and actors, particularly the news media and their journalists, on the one hand, and social networking sites and ordinary media users, on the other. This hybridization of affect circulation in such events is illustrated by the intense remediation of images of ritual gatherings, practices and representations in both news and social media. The greater the number of images and messages of public mourning circulated in the media, the more powerful the social image of the event's significance and the appropriate emotional response to the event.

Yet it is not only the dynamics between different media platforms and actors, but also the practices themselves that are affected by hybridization. The case in point here is the ritual. In the *Charlie Hebdo* media event, traditional offline ritual behaviours collided with online ritual actions. In these encounters, rituals always change as old and new elements converge and new layers and elements of practice are created. The circulation of a 'Je suis Charlie' meme, slogan or hashtag stands as a paradigmatic example of such behaviour that became profoundly ritualized in this media event. This type of hybridization of ritual practices shapes not only the narrative of the media event, but also those social and cultural assets that people can apply to engage with such events. To follow Dawes (2017), those emotional expressions ritualized in the media event may give ordinary social media users the opportunity to express opinions and feelings stirred up by the killings, and hence participate in the global media event. By doing so, they contribute to creating ephemeral and imagined communities around those structured and patterned expressions circulating in the social media. This, Dawes (2017, p. 184) suggests, may even call for collective action, to use the vocabulary of Bennett and Segerberg (2012), which has the power to shape the process of identity construction associated with the event at both the individual and the collective level (see also Badouard, 2016).

Chapter 6

Liveness and Acceleration of Circulation

One key dimension of a hybrid media event is the acceleration of circulation. The speed of communication makes and shapes the narrative and meaning-making of the event. Acceleration is tied with liveness, with the constant but uneven, and to some extent random coverage of events as they unfold. In this chapter, we discuss liveness and acceleration in the context of the *Charlie Hebdo* attacks. Just as more traditional media events in the mass media era, hybrid media events involve live broadcasting and live streaming (see also Sumiala et al., forthcoming). In contrast to mass media events, however, hybrid media events can be live broadcast and live streamed not only by professional news media, but also by various other actors: social media users, perpetrators and sometimes public officials, organizations and institutions. This multiplication of people streaming material has significant consequences for making and shaping the event, and it influences the narrative frames in which the event is given meaning. What is more, the live streaming of today's media events take place simultaneously in many spaces and on many media platforms. This can be called the intensification of liveness in today's media events (cf. Scannell, 2014). In this condition of intensified and simultaneous — accelerated — dissemination and circulation of information, our analysis of media events must be extended to incorporate new aspects.

The acceleration of circulation poses a major challenge not only for journalists and other media professionals, but also for public officials trying to handle an ongoing situation. It also provides new opportunities for both ordinary social media users and perpetrators to contribute to and interfere in shaping the event. That said, the accelerated circulation of messages and the conditions where actors are under constant live coverage have the power to shape the event inside out and outside in, which may also have implications for the outcomes and consequences of the event (cf. Cottle, 2014; Hjarvard, Mortensen, & Eskjær, 2015). Furthermore, it is important to acknowledge that these consequences may affect individuals and communities on different levels, from the individual to national and global level (cf. Hassan,

2009, p. 7). This influence is uneven and takes different forms in different localities and different media events.

In this chapter, we discuss liveness and the acceleration of circulation by analysing in some detail the acute phases of the two hostage situations that followed the *Charlie Hebdo* attacks. These situations, we argue, provide an example of the intensified workings of liveness in the event and thus provide valuable empirical material for exploring the implications of the acceleration of circulation in violent, hybrid media events. The *Charlie Hebdo* attacks culminated on Friday 9 January in two separate but connected hostage situations. One of them developed when the Kouachi brothers' escape was coming to an end, and the other one partly at the same time, when Amedy Coulibaly seized a kosher supermarket. Both of these violent situations involved multiple actors and media technologies, with both social media and professional news media contributing to the acceleration of circulation in the events. In our thick description of the events, we focus on three interwoven threads: the live broadcasting and streaming by professional media, the issue of hidden hostages and the mediated actions of the attackers.

6.1. Hostage Situation in Dammartin-en-Goële

After a two-day manhunt, the Kouachi brothers were chased on Friday morning to an industrial complex in Dammartin-en-Goële, a town of 8,500 people near the Charles de Gaulle airport. At 9 a.m., the Kouachis forced themselves into a printworks and took the owner, Michel Catalano, hostage. Catalano had recognized the heavily armed brothers and managed to tell his graphic designer Lilian Lepère to go and hide; he had stalled the brothers and given Lepère enough time to hide under the sink in a small closet. In the building, the Kouachis also encountered two other men, the factory manager and a salesman, but had let them go. 'We don't kill civilians', one of the brothers had said. The brothers soon asked Catalano whether there was anyone else in the building. Catalano said no, thinking Lepère would have a better chance of surviving if the brothers didn't know he was there. Catalano also offered to treat one of the brothers' neck wound, all the while hoping they would not find Lepère. The Kouachis did look around, but found no one. This left the brothers under the impression that they had one hostage — unaware that Lepère was hiding in the kitchen. In an interview with the British tabloid the *Daily Mail* on

Sunday 10 January,[1] Michel Catalano said: 'They asked me very calmly if they could have some water and I was trying to be cool so I said I could make them some coffee.' Police helicopters and armed troops arrived just a few minutes later, and surrounded the printworks. Locals were told to stay indoors and turn off their lights. Schoolchildren at an infant and primary school nearby were quickly evacuated. After a while, Chérif Kouachi told Michel Catalano to call the security forces and tell them he was being held hostage — and used as a human shield to protect France's most wanted fugitives. The Kouachis also opened the door and shouted to the security forces not to shoot because they had a hostage. After an hour, at 10 a.m., the brothers freed Michel Catalano, while Lepère remained in his hideout.

The media later reported the dramatic moments. On Monday 12 January Lepère said to the national broadcaster France 2: 'If I made even the smallest movement, either the doors would open on one side, or I would hit the wall on the other side.' He went on to describe how close a call his survival had been, as at one point one of the brothers approached his hiding place, started opening cabinet doors and took a drink from the tap in the sink under which Lepère was hiding. 'I could hear the water running just next to my head, I could see his shadow through the crack between the doors', Lepère recounted. 'The sink leaks, so I started to feel water running across my back. It was surreal. I was thinking this is like the movies, this only happens in movies' (Lepère, 12 January 2015[2]; *The Huffington Post*, 13 January 2015).[3] He told the media that immediately after hiding himself, he had texted to his father: 'I am hidden on the first floor. I think they have killed everyone. Tell the police to intervene.' Lepère's father had contacted the police and from then on, for more than eight hours, Lepère was in constant contact by phone with the police and was able to relay information to them about the movements and discussions of the Kouachi brothers (*Daily Mail*, 10 January 2015). Information about the hostage

---

[1]http://www.dailymail.co.uk/news/article-2904581/Owner-printers-held-hostage-dramatic-siege-Kouachi-brothers-dressed-terrorists-wounds-COFFEE-reveals-insists-s-sorry-died.html (Retrieved 18 September 2017).

[2]https://www.youtube.com/watch?time_continue=1&v=w5Psw056JEw (Retrieved 3 November 2017).

[3]https://www.huffingtonpost.com/2015/01/13/lilian-lepere-charlie-hebdo_n_6465872.html (Retrieved 18 September 2017).

situation had thus reached the police almost immediately after the Kouachis had entered the building.

The massive police operation against the Kouachis at the printworks was quickly followed by equally massive media attention. As both national French and international media agencies had been covering the attack and the manhunt in real time for two days, since Wednesday, they were able to quickly make their way to Dammartin-en-Goële. The town was soon swamped by journalists and cameramen and all their equipment. One of the many international media agencies that rushed to the scene was Russia Today (RT). Their journalist Peter Oliver started his live voice report in Russia Today's news (9 January 2015)[4] by saying: 'It is absolute chaos, the media are here from all over the world. [They] have descended on this small town.' He then proceeded to describe how the police had cut off all traffic in and out of the village: 'The police are moving reluctant journalists to this area where we are right now, we ourselves were moved from the site where we were planning to set up. But what we can see here now is that the whole world's media have descended on this small village and are trying to get shots, trying to get images of […] these gunmen.' He rounded up his report by assuring that RT was going to find out 'as much as possible, as soon as possible', and that they are going to 'go live with footage as soon as we possibly can'. This excerpt clearly illustrates the strength of the professional media presence on the scene and their ability and preparedness to broadcast live. This preparedness was similar to the pre-social media era. What was different was the variety of media outlets that travelled to the scene, focusing their attention on these cases and providing material for constant live streaming. It also goes to show that even the police had to take this media presence into account during their operation. In addition to live TV and radio broadcasts, journalists were constantly updating live blogs, Twitter feeds and Facebook pages, interviewing locals and writing stories about the school evacuation and searching for new angles from which to shoot the printworks. Most of the TV and radio broadcasts were also streamed through the internet.

The siege in Dammartin-en-Goële continued all day. During this time, information about the situation inside the printworks was leaked to the public via the intervention of the news media. Reporting for the French news network BFM TV, journalist Igor Sahiri managed to get an interview at 9 a.m. by calling the printworks where Chérif Kouachi

---

[4]https://www.youtube.com/watch?v=XDG_8P1n9R4 (Retrieved 18 September 2017).

answered the phone. The interview lasted less than two minutes, but in it Chérif Kouachi claimed he had connections with al-Qaeda in Yemen.

> *Chérif Kouachi*: I just want to tell you that we are defenders of the Prophet. I, Chérif Kouachi, was sent by al-Qaeda in Yemen. I was over there. I was financed by Imam Anwar al-Awlaki.
>
> *Journalist*: OK. How long ago, roughly?
>
> *Kouachi*: A long time ago. Before he was killed.
>
> *Journalist*: OK, so you came back to France recently.
>
> *Kouachi*: No, a long time ago. I had to know how I could do things properly.
>
> *Journalist*: Are you just there with your brother?
>
> *Kouachi*: That's not your problem.
>
> *Journalist*: Do you have other people there with you?
>
> *Kouachi*: That's not your problem.
>
> *Journalist*: Do you intend to kill again in the name of Allah. Or not?
>
> *Kouachi*: Have we killed other people in the last few days when you were looking for us? Go on. Tell me [...][5]

According to *The Independent* (10 January 2015),[6] the French BFM TV immediately shared the interview with the police, and did not broadcast it until after the siege was over. However, the crucial fact that a printworks employee, Lilian Lepère was hiding in the building was revealed to the public while the siege was still ongoing. At around 11:30 a.m., the National Assembly member for the area gave out the information in an interview to radio RMC, saying live on air that 'There is a person hiding in the warehouse.' This claim was immediately

---

[5]http://www.independent.co.uk/news/world/europe/paris-attackers-gave-interview-to-french-tv-station-we-are-defenders-of-the-prophet-we-took-9969749.html (Retrieved 18 September 2017).
[6]http://www.independent.co.uk/news/world/europe/paris-attackers-gave-interview-to-french-tv-station-we-are-defenders-of-the-prophet-we-took-9969749.html (Retrieved 18 September 2017).

repeated by two of France's largest television networks, TF1 and France 2. At 1 p.m., France 2 interviewed Lepère's sister in a live broadcast; she confirmed that her brother was believed to be in the building (BBC News, 18 August 2015).[7] She also said that 'he does not answer and we stopped calling', out of fear as that his safety may be compromised. The interview with Lepère's sister drew empathy from the viewers. One of them tweeted, 'The poor sister of the hostage on Fr2, and all his family. I hope he will do well. It makes you think'.

As reports of a hidden employer began to circulate in the media, his safety was indeed compromised. Rumours of hostages, their number, gender, age and relation to the printworks were rife on Twitter and other social media, and in live blogs published throughout the day. One of the tweets said: 'New reports say that Dammartin hostage is a 26-year-old man. This is unconfirmed. Earlier reports suggest a woman.'

The situation in Dammartin-en-Goële ended at around 5 p.m. when the Kouachis stormed out of the building, firing their guns. They were killed by security forces. And after more than eight hours in hiding, Lepère was finally able to come out from the cupboard, unharmed. After a psychological assessment, he was re-united with his family. It was by sheer luck that the Kouachis did not come across the information of Lepère's presence in the printworks during the hostage situation. This may have saved his life.

The live media feed from the Dammartin-en-Goële hostage situation was a complex and multilayered web of communication involving multiple actors, including professional news media, social media users, hostages, perpetrators and public officials such as the police. Our attention is particularly drawn to the live and intensified interplay between the news media and the perpetrators, and to the active role that journalists assumed in contacting the killers live. This situation also echoes the argument by Elihu Katz and Tamar Liebes (2007) that in disruptive media events, news media begin to serve the perpetrators' agenda by providing them a platform for delivering their message.

Many aspects of the second hostage situation in the kosher supermarket were similar to those seen in Dammartin-en-Goële. The key actors were the same (although different individuals), and included news media, hostages, the police, social media users and a perpetrator. Amedy Coulibaly was even better prepared than the Kouachi brothers in creating liveness: he had a GoPro video camera attached to his body

---

[7]http://www.bbc.com/news/world-europe-33983599 (Retrieved 18 September 2017).

to document and stream his actions in the supermarket. The next section describes in detail the siege at the kosher supermarket.

6.2.   The Kosher Market Siege

On the same day, that is 9 January, another hostage standoff began at around 12:30 p.m. in east Paris. Media and communication technology was again involved, in various ways. A third gunman, Amedy Coulibaly, seized a Jewish supermarket, filming his rampage using a GoPro video camera. The first 7 minutes and 45 seconds of the attack were recorded, showing how Coulibaly killed three people during the first seven minutes (Lazard & Le Bailly, 26 February 2016). One person who had tried to stop him was killed a bit later, and altogether 19 people were taken hostage. During the chaos, some shoppers were able to flee downstairs to a cold store, with the help of a shop assistant, Lassana Bathily, a Malian-born Muslim. In the meantime, Coulibaly had figured out that more people must be in hiding, so he sent another shop assistant downstairs to tell them to come up or everyone will be shot. According to *The Guardian* (19 August 2015),[8] at least one man with his three-year-old son came back upstairs, while others remained in their freezing hiding place. Lassana then decided to escape using the delivery lift. At first the police thought he was an assailant, but when they learned he was in fact a witness, they gained valuable information about the situation inside the store. Six hostages remained in the cold store, where the temperature was minus three degrees Celsius, while several others were upstairs with the perpetrator.

The hostages upstairs later told the media that Coulibaly had tried during the siege to use his computer to connect to the internet. Having failed, he forced a hostage to help him get online to access the news and to upload his footage (Brenner, August 2015). Though the French investigators have viewed the footage later and *Le Nouvel Observateur* published a transcription of the video on February 2015, it has remained unclear whether Coulibaly managed to share the material online during

---

[8]https://www.theguardian.com/world/2015/aug/19/charlie-hebdo-hostage-sues-french-media-for-putting-his-life-in-danger (Retrieved 18 September 2017).

the seige (Pelletier, 30 January 2015[9]; CNN, 31 January 2015[10]; Lazard & Le Bailly, 26 January 2015[11]).

During the siege, Coulibaly also spoke to the media. According to CNN (11 January 2015),[12] French radio station RTM had called the kosher market after the authorities had announced that customers and workers had been taken hostage. Coulibaly spoke briefly on the phone, but then failed to hang up the old-fashioned landline phone and the radio station was able to record what he said to the hostages. This allowed the media and the police to hear him and to learn about his movements. According to *The Independent* (10 January 2015),[13] Coulibaly himself called BMF TV at around 3 p.m. on one of his hostage's phones and spoke to the deputy news editor. He demanded that the police release the Kouachi brothers, who were still in the printworks surrounded by security forces. In this interview, Coulibaly claimed that he and the Kouachi brothers had synchronized their operations. BFM TV broadcast an extract from this interview while the siege was still ongoing, and revealed other details as well.

The police gleaned information from within the kosher market via other channels, too. The people who were hiding in the cold room had sent text messages to relatives and the police. Some family members who knew their relatives were probably being held in the kosher market also contacted the police. This information helped police track the location of the hostages and take that into consideration as they planned to storm the store. According to *The Independent* (9 January 2015),[14] the authorities managed to hack the shop's CCTV camera and watch the situation as it unfolded in the store. However, as happened in

---

[9]http://www.lexpress.fr/actualite/societe/enquete/coulibaly-a-envoye-les-images-de-la-tuerie-de-l-hyper-cacher_1646812.html (Retrieved 3 November 2017).

[10]http://edition.cnn.com/2015/01/10/world/france-market-shooting-scene/index.html (Retrieved 18 September 2017).

[11]http://tempsreel.nouvelobs.com/charlie-hebdo/20150225.OBS3345/levez-vous-ou-j-vais-vous-allumer-la-video-macabre-de-l-hyper-cacher.html (Retrieved 3 November 2017).

[12]https://edition.cnn.com/2015/01/10/world/france-market-shooting-scene/index.html

[13]http://www.independent.co.uk/news/world/europe/paris-attackers-gave-interview-to-french-tv-station-we-are-defenders-of-the-prophet-we-took-9969749.html   (Retrieved 18 September 2017).

[14]http://www.independent.co.uk/news/world/europe/paris-shootings-how-sieges-at-d ammartin-en-goele-print-works-and-jewish-grocer-ended-9968962.html   (Retrieved 18 September 2017).

Dammartin-en-Goële, information about the hidden hostages soon became public, while the siege was still going on. It was a BFM TV journalist who reported live on air: 'There's a person, a woman, who might have been hiding from the start in the fridge. And who is probably still there.'

As in Dammartin-en-Goële, some 45 kilometres from the kosher supermarket at Port-au-Vincennes, the broadcasting media had set up their equipment to follow the unfolding hostage situation on the ground and were reporting and broadcasting the events live. Television cameras filmed across the street how Coulibaly made his final charge and ran out of the supermarket, firing gunshots. French police special forces, the *Groupe d'Intervention de la Gendarmerie Nationale* (GIGN), created after the deadly failure to counter the hostage taking of Israeli Olympians at the 1972 Games in Munich, shot him down just minutes after the Kouachi brothers were killed. Soon, the media were filled with videos and images of terrified hostages evacuated from the store. During the weekend, images taken by the hostages themselves of their ordeal in the freezer room started to circulate, together with images captured from the supermarket's CCTV cameras. Although he had been shot dead, Amedy Coulibaly re-appeared during that same weekend, when a 7.16-minute video narrating his suicide mission emerged online. Entitled 'Soldier of the Caliphate', the 'martyrdom video' was, according to *The Guardian* (11 January 2015),[15] originally 'circulated by propagandists working for the extremist Islamic group'. However, it was only discovered and reported by online media on Sunday 11 January, just hours before the start of the unity march in Paris, which was attended by several world leaders. The Guardian (11 January 2015) explains that the skilfully edited video was partly filmed following the massacre at the *Charlie Hebdo* offices on Wednesday, but before Coulibaly's attack on Friday. In the video, Coulibaly appears in various guises, and he claims his siege was connected to the Kouachi brothers' attack. Video material was also included that showed the police storming the kosher supermarket and gunning down Coulibaly. In other words, the video must have been produced after his death, yet it remains unclear who filmed and edited it.

---

[15]https://www.theguardian.com/world/2015/jan/11/paris-supermarket-attacker-islamic-state-video-isis-amedy-coulibaly (Retrieved 18 September 2017).

6.2.1.   Live Broadcasting Puts Hostages in Danger

As discussed above, the dynamics activated in the live broadcasting and streaming of the kosher market siege was similar to that seen in the Dammartin-en-Goële situation. The news media appeared on the site almost immediately and began broadcasting live on their news channels and streaming on online sites. There was also active communication between the perpetrator and the news media.

Coulibaly furthermore had a very carefully planned media strategy, including the use of a GoPro video camera, direct contact with the news media and his martyr video. All these aspects increased his presence in the live performance of the hostage situation and drew public attention to himself and his message. In this way, the perpetrator's deliberate use of liveness and knowledge of the workings of professional media helped to make him a protagonist in the news media narrative and resulted in the news media actually furthering his agenda. The hostages in hiding also had an important role. Their exchange of mobile messages with family members was soon picked up by the news media, and some of the live broadcasts referred to the situation of the hostages in the building. This intensified liveness jeopardized the lives of the hostages: there was a very real risk that the perpetrators might have learned from the news where the hostages were hiding.

6.3.   The Aftermath

The liveness of the event had consequences for journalistic media and illustrates the close connection between terrorists and media. The news media's desire for real-time images and information affected the efforts of the police, put the hostages at risk and caused moral outrage among audiences. According to French police, they were constantly calling media houses throughout the operation to discourage them from asking for eyewitness photos and to prevent them from phoning the attackers or the victims (Ehrhard & Garrier, 2015). They also issued instructions for journalists working in social media. In an appeal to the news agencies, they tweeted: 'Dear journalists, avoid filming the premises in order to avoid communicating the locations of police forces.' The decision by the news media to interview the attackers and so to give them exposure caused some anger, too. In reaction, the police tweet was extensively retweeted by ordinary people. Individuals retweeting this message also mentioned the Twitter user accounts of BFM TV, France 2 and other media agencies in their messages. This way people wanted to make sure the media outlets received the police message. In several cases, police messages were accompanied by uppercase warnings not to deliver any information to the assassins. Some commentators went so far as to describe BFM TV in particular as the terrorists' accomplice: 'Thank you media for passing on tactical information to the terrorists.'

In other words, the liveness of the event was intensified because the perpetrators spoke with journalists and were given air-time. The fact that the media hanged on every word coming from the attackers, always eager to be the first to publish and broadcast any morsel of new information relating to the unfolding event, contributed to the accelerated circulation of information and misinformation. The audience, too, was in a constant state of crisis preparedness (cf. Frosh & Pinchevski, 2009), ready to participate in the event by commenting on and sharing and shaping every bit of new information.

On 12 February 2015, France's broadcasting watchdog, the Conseil superieur de l'audiovisuel (CSA) issued formal warnings to 16 French television and radio stations. CSA found 36 breaches, some of which were considered to have put the lives of the hostages in danger by revealing sensitive information during the ongoing hostage situations. In general, the watchdog criticized the live broadcasting and streaming of information and images from the printworks and the kosher supermarket while the hostages were still being held. More specifically, it blamed the media for revealing live on air that people were hiding in the buildings, which clearly put at risk the lives of the hostages. Other criticisms concerned the live broadcasting of images and information of the confrontation with the Kouachi brothers, while Coulibaly was still entrenched in Porte de Vincennes. The live broadcasts from Dammartin-en-Goële endangered the lives of the hostages in the kosher market: Coulibaly had specifically demanded that the Kouachi brothers be allowed to walk free or he would kill his hostages. All three attackers in the two separate locations were in touch with the media. The Kouachi brothers had smartphones and a radio and could have easily found out about Lepère's presence from media reports. Amedy Coulibaly, too, was in contact with journalists and used the internet during the siege, and could have learned about the hidden hostages and the police attacking the Kouachis. Fortunately — and quite miraculously — for the hostages, none of this information circulating in the media reached the perpetrators.

Broadcasters responded defiantly to the CSA's criticisms, which in the words of Thierry Thuillier from the state-run France Televisions group 'raised major questions over the right to inform in our country' (RFI, 13 February 2015).[16] Head of BFM TV news Hervé Béroud referred to the substantial commitment of manpower and technology that was required when covering a violent media event: 'We put out 70 hours live broadcasting non-stop in January. There was one mistake of 23 seconds, when we revealed that there were people in the cold room' (BBC News, 28 August 2015).[17] All in all the news editors of 14 TV and radio channels, both private and public, contested CSA's criticisms and wrote a joint letter titled 'Information under threat'. They asked: 'How is it possible to think that, in 2015, the CSA wishes to reinforce the control on an already regulated French broadcasting media while information circulates without constraint in the written press, on foreign channels, all social media and websites? [...] How in the light of these sanctions can we continue to inform?' (Mapping Media Freedom, 21 August 2015[18]; BBC News, 28 August 2015[19])

In April 2015, a group of people who had been hiding in the Jewish supermarket initiated a lawsuit against French media outlets that had revealed their location during the siege. According to the group's lawyer, Patrick Klugman, the victims 'could have been at risk if Coulibaly had been aware in real time what BFM TV was broadcasting', noting furthermore that Coulibaly had been watching news reports during the siege. He also stated that 'the working methods of media in real time in this type of situation were tantamount to goading someone to commit a crime' (*Sputnik International*, 3 April 2015).[20]

In July 2015, Lilian Lepère also sued the media for endangering his life. At least two of France's largest television networks, France 2 and TF1, and radio station RMC revealed that someone was hiding in the building on 9 January 2015. Lepère's lawyer referred to the problems raised by live media coverage: 'The divulging of information in real time, while the Kouachi brothers — armed and dangerous — were able to follow how the operation was going, presented a real risk to Lilian.' The Paris prosecutor's office opened preliminary investigations on both

---

[16]http://en.rfi.fr/culture/20150213-french-broadcasters-protest-official-criticism-char lie-hebdo-coverage (Retrieved 18 September 2017).
[17]http://www.bbc.com/news/world-europe-34071842 (Retrieved 18 September 2017).
[18]https://mappingmediafreedom.org/plus/index.php/2015/08/21/lawsuit-takes-french-media-to-task-for-charlie-hebdo-reporting/ (Retrieved 18 September 2017).
[19]http://www.bbc.com/news/world-europe-34071842 (Retrieved 18 September 2017).
[20]https://sputniknews.com/europe/201504031020421891/ (Retrieved 18 September 2017).

cases (BBC News, 18 August 2015).[21] However, in 2016, the hostages of the Kosher market dropped the charges as BFM TV donated 60,000 euros to an association supporting victims of terrorist violence (Fond social juif unifié). Furthermore, the channel stated on its website that in the future cases of hostage situation, they will do their best not to endanger the hostages and will honour the hostages and their families (*Le Monde*, 8 January 2016).

6.4. Acceleration of Circulation in a Hybrid Media Event

Our two empirical examples of the hostage situations in the wake of the *Charlie Hebdo* attacks are intended to illustrate the complex processes and dynamics of acceleration in hybrid media events. The examples show how those process not only shaped the meanings and interpretations of the event, but also how media outlets became participants in the event. In addition, the consequences of liveness are apparent at several levels. First, the intensified liveness speeded up communication between the different parties in the event, including professional news media, the perpetrators, ordinary social media users, hostages and their family members and the police who were involved in the rescue operation. Second, this accelerated circulation of information, the sharing and remediation of messages via mobile and online media technologies, exposed the hostage situation: it was possible to follow in real time what was happening on the spot, and this information could be immediately aired and shared in online media. At the same time, the complexity of information brought great confusion and disorder. Unconfirmed and inaccurate information was being circulated both in the news and social media, alongside confirmed and accurate information, and it was extremely difficult to separate the facts from the non-facts.

Third, the accelerated circulation of contents made it difficult to create solid narrative frames to make sense of the event. As things were happening while being broadcast live, and indeed being transformed because of the live streaming, there was no clear storyline. We could call this a moment of hybridization of narrative structures and frames. It was only after the episode, once the perpetrators had been killed, that the connection between the two hostage situations became more firmly established. Fourth, the intensified liveness of a hybrid media event

---

[21]http://www.bbc.com/news/world-europe-33983599 (Retrieved 18 September 2017).

creates a disaster marathon (Katz & Liebes, 2007) that compels all types of media users to follow and to participate to the point that it may be described as addictive. The constant stream of updates and new information continues to introduce new players, angles and perspectives in the event, transforming it into a real-life thriller which everyone with digital access can take part in and contribute to.

Fifth, we argue that liveness and the accelerated circulation of incohesive information in a constantly changing condition serves the interests of the perpetrators. In a situation where information is constantly in flux, fed by countless communicative actions of countless actors, the perpetrators' message begins to appear rather constant and well-defined. This will make it appealing not only for the news media trying to make sense of the episode and competing for audience attention, but also for individual social media users. As events were unfolding, then, the audience may still have had no idea what was going on in Dammartin-en-Goële or in the kosher market, but they may have understood why and for what purpose the killers were doing what they were. In this frame of thinking, the intensified liveness and acceleration of circulation in a hybrid media event gives increased recognition to the activities and motivations of the perpetrators, making those motivations a key element of this media event.

Sixth and finally, we wish to address the issue of ethics in connection with the acceleration of liveness in a hybrid media event. In the two hostage situations we have described, real lives were put at risk. All those involved in making the media event should therefore bear moral responsibility for their communicative actions. The question we need to ask is this: Should broadcasters refrain from publishing information and images that are being circulated in social media? One answer is offered by Hervé Bérrou, BFM TV's head of news: 'If the responsible, organized media — the ones with chains of command and professional reporters — if they are the ones who are punished and made to self-censor, then what will happen is that viewers will go elsewhere: to the social media and the internet, where there is no control on content whatsoever.'

This is a common argument of news outlets, who claim it is unjust that regulations and sanctions only apply to corporations defined as national media organizations. In this context, the amplifying effect and liveness of broadcasting media is often conveniently forgotten. Although the concern of broadcasting companies is understandable in that the growth of hybridity in the media environment has made for more complex and asymmetrical regulation in relation to different producers and contents, it is in fact the liveness produced by those companies that amplifies social media messages and that accelerate circulation. As discussed in Chapter 3 on actors and affordances, it is clear that those who already have fame or professional access to media will gain the most attention. No individual Twitter user would have been able to spread the perpetrators' message as widely as professional television and radio did.

However, there is no denying the importance of this issue. Bérrou claims that social media users should also assume responsibility for their actions in the heated moments of hostage situations that are streamed live. This also ties in with the question of the responsibility of the global social media platforms where the contents circulate. This hybridization of moral responsibility in today's violent global media events is a theme we address in more detail in the final chapter of our book.

Chapter 7

Charlie Hebdo and the Circulation of Terrorist Violence in a Hybrid Media Event

The purpose of this book has been to contribute to the research on violent media events by theoretically and empirically developing the concept of hybrid in the context of contemporary media events. In the beginning of the book, we discussed the key debates around the development of media event theory. The three nodal points in those debates were (1) ceremonial and/or disruptive media events and their social consequences aimed at cohesion and/or distraction; (2) the changes occurring in the media environment, particularly the shift from televisual media events embedded in the communicative logic of transmission to digital media events embedded in complex interactions between news media and social media and (3) the aspect of time in the narrative construction of the event, particularly the dynamics between 'live' media events experienced here and now, and 'mnemonic schemes' of interpretation (Zelizer, 2018) that shape this experience and the way this 'now' is made sense of.

We maintain that while the hybrid media event as a theoretical construct shares many features in common with earlier theoretical constructs of ceremonial and/or disruptive media events in the television era, the premises of media event theory and the empirical appearance and consequences of media events in society have been profoundly affected by changes in the media environment. Looking at the continuities in the way that media events are understood, we find that all events stem from interruptions of daily routines; that they are communicated in live broadcasting or streaming and that they are intended to address large audiences on screens. Furthermore, it is noteworthy that both ceremonial and disruptive events can still be found, and that ceremoniality and disruption can co-occur, as happened in Finland when a group of anarchists staged violent demonstrations during televised independence day celebrations in 2013 (Heikka, Valaskivi, & Uskali, 2016). All media events aim to establish an effect that Dayan and Katz (1992) described by saying the 'whole world is watching,' and all media events have normative prospects with regard to their audience (i.e. they impose participation).

Apart from these fairly obvious continuities between media events that took place before the age of network media and those now taking place in the hybrid media environment, our work in this book has identified some key discontinuities and changes in media events. First, the logics constituting these events have changed with the advent of digitalized, network media. In other words, the media environment has changed, and the ways in which both ceremonial and disruptive events take place have changed and become hybridized. These changes, we argue, have further implications for the consequences of media events in today's mediatized world. While pre-network media events were scripted by professional journalists, political and social elites and at times by violent attackers, today's hybrid media events are created in a complex circulation of different actors, platforms and representations that no individual party can single-handedly control. This change can be described as a shift from transmission to networked constitution of and in media events. What is more, this multiplicity of actors and platforms and the circulation of representations in hybrid media events is characteristically transnational, or even global, as are its implications. We return to this issue towards the end of this chapter.

But in order for the concept of 'hybrid' to become more than just a buzzword in describing today's violent media events, we still need to delve into its qualities and features in relation to media and media events. It was to this end that we developed the five A's (actors, affordances, attention, affect, acceleration) as our analytical tool. In the introduction, we explained that our approach to the concept of hybrid takes inspiration from three scholars in the field, namely Bruno Latour, Marwan M. Kraidy and Andrew Chadwick. From Latour (1993), we borrowed the idea of hybrid encounters between human and non-human actors, and argued that in hybrid media events this interaction between individuals, institutions, discourses and technology plays a crucial role in constituting their networked character. In the case of the *Charlie Hebdo* attacks, communication in and about the attacks was heavily influenced by the close interplay on social media (in this case Twitter) between individual and institutional actors (not only media company accounts and other institutional accounts, but also journalists, politicians, police, ordinary media users and even the perpetrators), and this interplay therefore also contributed to shaping the event narrative. One of the most apparent examples of this intensified circulation of messages between different actors was provided by the two hostage situations which ended in the deaths of all three perpetrators. In Chapter 3, we empirically analysed in more detail the complex interplay between different actors in connection with affordance and argued for a close interdependence between the two. The messages of actors who have high attention value to start with (such as well-known media institutions, celebrities or individuals who emerge as key actors in certain situations such as the hostage standoff) are bound to attract more interest in this hybrid media environment. As a result, the circulation of messages sent by highly valued actors are more likely to become accelerated in communication.

Marwan Kraidy's (2005) work on hybridity proved useful in our analysis of symbolic modes of communication created around performances of solidarity (e.g., 'Je suis Charlie') and the countless responses from different actors on different media platforms. In addition to those hybrid cultural modes of communication, Kraidy's work points to the ongoing imbalances in power relations and the simplified oppositions between 'the West' and 'the rest' in this communication. These imbalances became highly visible in the *Charlie Hebdo* attacks. To put it simply, as discussed in Chapter 5, the media narrative around the public 'Je suis Charlie' demonstrations of solidarity repeated the story of a 'civilized' and 'secular' West and the threat presented by religious Islam to the West and its values, particularly freedom of speech. Although 'Je suis Charlie' was not the only narrative circulating in the media after the attacks, it was associated with strong emotional responses and reactions, which again intensified its circulation.

Andrew Chadwick's (2013) idea of hybrid media system takes our analysis to the level of the media environment and the complex interplay between different media. Following Chadwick, we paid special attention to the ways in which the narratives around *Charlie Hebdo* were created in a complex interaction between the news media and social media. This was particularly apparent in the circulation of the message and slogan 'Je suis Charlie', first tweeted by journalist Joachim Ronchin (see Chapter 3), and the amateur video material of the killing of police officer Ahmed Merabet filmed by Jordi Mir (see Chapter 4). This intensified dynamic in the circulation of messages between news and social media in the present hybrid media environment also amplified the social, political and cultural relevance of this event.

7.1.   Circulation Connects Key Elements

It is important to note that hybridity is a result of multiple interactions and connections between the five elements of hybridity in media events. These five elements are tied together by a sixth element that is processes of circulation, a concept we have used in this book descriptively to highlight the dynamics of movement between the different parties involved in the event. Elsewhere (e.g. Sumiala, 2008; Valaskivi & Sumiala, 2014, pp. 44–55), we have argued that in its simplest form, circulation is about 'going around' and/or 'passing on' something that is being distributed and disseminated. This 'something' can include material and immaterial items as well as human and non-human actors. It is also useful to think about circulation as a spiral or cyclone. The movement of ideas and actors is not steady or circular in the sense that they continue to move around the same circle over and over again (see also Valaskivi & Sumiala, 2014, p. 231). Instead, circulation is driven by a centrifugal force that draws elements into the whirl. In our analysis of the *Charlie Hebdo* attacks, we demonstrated how certain affordances direct attention to certain messages (e.g. the video of the death of Ahmed Merabet), and how these messages absorb affective energies that again stimulate their circulation. In this process, ideas about the death of Ahmed Merabet and their value in the story of the *Charlie Hebdo* attacks become more powerful, and other incidents without such interplay between actors and media technologies — affordances — are diminished or even left out of circulation, which means that they tend to fade away or change. The deaths of the two other police officers killed in the attacks serve as examples of such weakened circulation.

But as Benjamin Lee and Edward LiPuma (2002, pp. 191–192) remind us, circulation is not only about the movement of actors, ideas and messages. It is also a cultural process created by interactions between specific types of circulating forms and interpretive communities, social entities that have the capacity to set out lines of interpretation and to specify boundaries to circulation based on their own internal dynamics (see also Sumiala & Tikka, 2011, p. 255). Key outcomes of this cultural process include the shared imaginations of belonging created in those circulations. Or, as Mark Allen Peterson (2005, p. 256) maintains, this sense of togetherness is based on imagining others similar to oneself engaging in media practices like those in which one is engaged oneself. This is how imagination experienced and lived through in different media contexts works as a symbolic matrix within which people imagine their collective social life in such media events.

In hybrid media events, circulation is relevant to all five A's. The actors and their relationship with the media environment define how and what kind of material is circulated. This relationship is based on affordances: the ways in which technological properties are socially utilized in the media event. Our empirical analysis confirms earlier findings (cf. Sumiala & Tikka, 2011) that affective, sticky (Ahmed, 2004a, 2004b) contents and meanings are the most spreadable, drawing attention in circulation and gaining more symbolic power as they circulate. The accelerated circulation of contents and the accumulation of attention cause reliance on well-established frames and metonymic connections that in our case relate to the dichotomy between Islam and the West and definitions of terrorism.

Circulation, then, is the dynamic through which things and ideas are collectively imagined. As long as something gains attention in circulation, it will only cease to exist when the circulation stops. It follows that the only way it is possible to change our collective imagining of terrorist violence and related power relations is by refocusing our attention to the elements of circulation and narratives in circulation.

7.2. Towards a Discussion of the Social and Ethical Dimensions of Hybrid Media Events

A terrorist attack disrupts the course of everyday life, and calls for rituals to restore ordinariness. In this type of condition, it is understandable that the media is keen to try and find explanations and meanings for what has happened. However, as we have demonstrated in this book, the difficulty in today's hybrid media events of terrorist violence lies in the accelerated circulation of certain emotions and the reliance on mnemonic schemes that date back to 9/11 and even earlier (see, e.g., Zelizer, 2018). In these schemes, bodies and cultural references are attached to particular affects. In the hybrid media event, interpretation takes place in an instant: the first interpretations are offered even before the events have run their course, or the perpetrator is known, or apprehended. The *Charlie Hebdo* attacks activated a narrative and related symbols that reinforced the sense of community of 'the West', the free world. In this case the ultimate symbol of the West was freedom of speech, which prompted politicians, journalists and citizens to join in, not only in tweeting 'Je suis Charlie', but also in demonstrations in support of freedom of speech. This narrative then drew counter-narratives and reactions commenting and opposing it.

This is where our focus must lie if we want to understand the consequences of hybrid media events of terrorist violence: we need to concentrate on narratives of and around terrorism. Cristina Archetti (2012, p. 91) points out that '[...] terrorist action is the outcome of the constitution of an identity and a corresponding narrative that legitimizes violent action'. If we want to understand and unravel the role of mediated communication in terrorism and find ways to do better, we need to understand the circulation of narratives of terrorism and particularly the ways in which imagining and circulating ideas about terrorism and defining terrorists contribute to violence.

In his book *Jihad and Death: The Global Appeal of Islamic State*, Olivier Roy (2016) discusses the presence of jihad in Europe. He pays particular attention to the issue of narratives around identities associated with terrorists and terrorism. Roy describes how 'the West' is a prisoner of its own fear of Islam. Its own narrative construction of a uniform, radical Islam that is at war with 'the West', Roy says, prevents it from seeing many relevant conditions behind contemporary jihadism in the West. Roy's analysis is based on his empirical work on data compiled in recent years about Belgian and French terrorists and their profiles. It also includes an examination of the Kouachi brothers and Amedy Coulibaly, three perpetrators who are discussed in this book.

In Roy's understanding, the jihadism seen in the Western contexts he has studied has a very particular relationship with Islam and fundamentalism and/or Salafism. Most of the radicalized jihadists Roy has studied have had rather superficial knowledge of Islam theology, very little Arabic, no religious education and no close connection with local mosques. Their lifestyles prior to radicalization have not been particularly pious. Rather, these young men have enjoyed drinking, taking drugs, partying and living promiscuous lives — none of which are acceptable for a pious Muslim, but more typical of the lifestyles of Western young adults.

The radicalized perpetrators studied by Roy came from disadvantaged backgrounds. Many of them were born in Europe, but lived in low-SES migrant neighbourhoods plagued with high unemployment. Many had done time in prison for petty crime. Roy (2016) concludes that this has played an important role in their radicalization, for the prison environment is conducive to the formation of networks of like-minded, frustrated, young Muslim men who are susceptible to radical jihadist propaganda.

In this setting, the propaganda of terrorist organizations such as al-Qaeda or ISIS/ISIL provides an attractive, religiously inspired narrative for these men — a narrative of loser turned hero. It promises a masculine identity grounded in revenge and rejection of the identity of their parents' generation who (in this narrative) were too submissive to Western rule and who therefore were unable to defend the honour of Muslim identity. The radicalization of these young men is not only directed against Western society and its purportedly dismissive attitude towards Islam, but also against their parents' generation and their surrendered identity. Paradoxically enough, the heroic identity that so appeals to the new recruits takes its inspiration from Western popular culture and its violent gaming images, for instance. Furthermore, Roy (2016) maintains that this radical masculine Muslim identity is death seeking and nihilistic. It is not so much inspired by the fantasy of a caliphate or paradise, but of death over life. In this sense, its take on terrorist propaganda (whether al-Qaeda or ISIS/ISIL) and terrorist organization is, in fact, very partial and eclectic as well as fragmental. Roy (2016) puts it that in some cases, drawing comparisons between radicalized jihadists and school shooters is not all that far-fetched. School shooters, too, are often characterized as nihilists and losers in society who crave for recognition and revenge. In both cases, the mass killings are carried out in a spectacular, highly mediatized manner (Muschert & Sumiala, 2012). And for both, the act of terror promises a narrative of loser turned hero, albeit usually postmortem. This narrative, we should not forget, is one of the most prominent narratives of contemporary popular culture.

To follow Cristina Archetti's (2012) explanation, terrorist action comes from the constitution of an identity and a corresponding narrative that legitimizes violent action. Identities are formed relationally, that is, in relation to other people, political power structures, ideologies — and in this particular instance in relation to media narratives created and circulated in a hybrid media event. We argued earlier in this book that narratives in hybrid media events are never created only in the present, or in a historical vacuum. The mnemonic scheme (Zelizer, 2018) in today's media events of terrorist violence is that of jihadist terrorism. In this post 9/11 media narrative, the interpretation is that Western democratic values are at variance with Islam, which is seen as the religion of terrorists. This media narrative is tied up with the affective economy in which every Muslim (young male) body is seen as a potential terrorist defined by religion and culture (Said, 1981/1997), whereas young white males who kill are simply seen as mentally imbalanced.

So strong is this metonymic connection between terrorism and Islam that when Anders Breivik in 2011 killed more than 70 people in Norway, newspapers in Nordic countries felt it necessary to point out that 'Not all terrorists are Muslims' (Hokka, Valaskivi, Sumiala, & Laakso, 2013). This narrative scheme in hybrid media events of terrorist violence that automatically produces Muslim men as 'terrorist' may thus in fact impose radicalization and violence on society.

7.3.   What Can Be Done?

In contemporary hybrid media events, the accelerated circulation of interpretations drives all actors to resort to metonymic, stereotypical connections and mnemonic schemes, even those who would wish to act differently. Is it possible to defy the weight of the collective narrative, to avoid political opportunism and try to alleviate the contradictions that feed into the fear that sustains terrorism? In *Media, Society, World: Social Theory and Digital Practice*, Nick Couldry (2012) mentions three ethical dimensions, that is, journalistic ethics, media ethics and communication ethics, that are all relevant to rethinking ethics in hybrid media events of terrorist violence. The accelerated pace of information and (mis)information circulation in hybrid media events, driven by fierce competition for audience attention, raises significant new ethical challenges for journalism. As news journalists in local, national and international media compete for scoops, they may sometimes fail to double-check their facts and sources and make sure those sources are protected. It is not uncommon that in the aftermath of violent media events, journalists and news media are accused of unethical conduct (see, e.g., Raittila, Koljonen, & Väliverronen, 2010). In the *Charlie Hebdo* attacks, these accusations stemmed from concerns over the safety of the hostages, when their whereabouts were disclosed while they were still in hiding from the terrorists. Lawsuits were initiated against some news media in France (e.g., BFM TV; see Chapter 6).

But it is no longer enough just to rethink the ethical codes of journalism. We also need to address what Nick Couldry (2012) refers to as media ethics and communication ethics. Based on our research, we argue that communication ethics — the ethics of everyone involved in communication — and media ethics in hybrid media events are thoroughly intertwined and inseparable and need to be discussed in concert with each other. Couldry's (2012) aim is to draft 'general' media ethics based on the smallest common denominators, so that the principles could be accepted and applied throughout the global media environment. The three key principles relevant for media ethics are (1) accuracy, (2) sincerity and (3) the virtue of care. Accuracy is about making the effort and using the resources necessary to make as sure as possible that the information distributed is correct and accurate. Closely related to accuracy is the principle of sincerity that is saying what one actually means as accurately as possible. The virtue of care, then, concerns everybody and anybody who is involved in communication, and requires that all actors involved in mediated communication — and in the formation of hybrid media events, for instance — care about the consequences of the circulation of the material they might produce. Care ties in with hospitality, which should be shown to all the 'others' represented in different media texts (Silverstone, 2007) and circulating media materials.

It is clear that future studies of global hybrid media events of terrorist violence will need to pay more attention not only to journalistic ethics, but also perhaps even more so to the aspects of media and communication ethics. We wish to conclude this book by asking what would it mean to consider and respect the principles of accuracy, sincerity and the virtue of care in the context of hybrid media event or terrorist violence? Once again, we must turn to the actors in hybrid media events. In hybrid media events of terrorist violence, no human party involved in the event, whether politician, professional news journalist, ordinary media user or official, can avoid responsibility for their actions in such an event. In a situation where a spectacle is unfolding in front of our eyes and on screen, it may be extremely difficult to cultivate and adhere to the ethical code of accurate, sincere and respectful communication, but this does not mean it should not be imposed and enforced on the actors involved. To follow Roger Silverstone's (2007) insight, the ethics of responsible communication in our digital media world is not just a matter for media houses and professional news media actors. It concerns all of us. Every click and every comment we post becomes a moral act, and we, ourselves, are responsible for it. This type of media and communication ethics is the ethics of individual level communication.

The issue of human agency in the framework of institutions and organizations raises another set of questions. These concern not only professional news media actors and media houses, but also politicians and the institutions they represent, as well as the police and other officials representing organized society. Institutional actors should consider the effects of their communicative actions that influence not only their organization, but also other institutions and organizations with which they are connected. A case in point is provided by police communication in global media events of terrorist violence. In the case of the *Charlie Hebdo* attacks, one challenging communicative situation emerged in two hostage situations in which multiple actors (the perpetrators, the media, hostages, their relatives and officials) were sending and sharing information, rumours and comments in the hybrid media environment. In this condition, communication on and around and a given situation becomes a crucial part of the operation. If we take seriously the idea that terrorism is an identity position supported by a narrative that permits violence, it is crucial to make this narrative less, not more attractive. This said, it is critical that institutional and collective actors in hybrid media events also recognize the potential consequences of their actions. The first step is to be conscious of the dimensions of the event. Actors need to be responsible in their media conduct and aware of the consequences of accelerated circulation, interpretation and reactions. This would also mean paying closer attention to affordances and developing technologies aimed at or based on public rather than business interests. This would mean taking seriously issues of social media moderation and opportunities for technology induced empathy development. Also, ethical, social and legal considerations would have to be incorporated in technology development from an earlier stage. Future research on hybrid media events of terrorist violence must pay more attention, then, to developing collective media and communication ethics in this hybrid media environment. This need has become ever more urgent in recent years with the escalation of conscious efforts to distort information, to manipulate users and voters and to circulate propaganda via digital media (Ventre, 2016).

Global hybrid media events of terrorist violence are triggered by radical violence. The ethical principles of communication — accuracy, sincerity and care — must therefore be thought of as communicative responses to destructive violence. As discussed in this book, emotions such as sadness, fear, anger and anxiety all play an important role in such situations and trigger a need to comment on and react to what is happening. Thus, we argue that future research on hybrid media events of terrorist violence must give more attention to how to develop media and communication ethics that has the ability to recognize and take into consideration those emotional undertones that generate communication in such events. This may require nurturing skills such as calming down, tolerating confusion without panicking and the art of listening (cf. Back, 2007) to others in such a disturbing condition, instead of rushing headlong to a judgmental conclusion before even knowing what has just happened — all skills that go against the grain of standard communication in a hybrid media event. After all, hybrid media events of terrorist violence are also illusions. They claim importance, globality and totality far beyond their actual reference point. Empirically speaking, the whole world was not watching Paris and not everyone claimed 'Je suis Charlie' when the attacks happened. This is not to downplay the pain and suffering of those who lost loved ones in the attacks or who felt insecure and anxious, but to remind us of the place and importance of such events in the broader context of life. Cultivating this thought may be the best way to oppose the hubris of today's hybrid media events of terrorist violence.

References

Abbott, A. (2001). *Time matters: On theory and method*. Chicago, IL: Chicago University Press.

AFP News Agency. (13 January 2015). Tributes paid to French Muslim policeman at burial. AFP News Agency. Retrieved from https://www.youtube.com/watch?v=26VgrG1nOvk

Ahmed, S. (2004a). *The cultural politics of emotion*. Edinburgh: Edinburgh University Press.

Ahmed, S. (2004b). Affective economies. *Social Text, 79, 22*(2), 117–139.

Al-Arian, A. (10 January 2015). *Charlie Hebdo* and western liberalism: Islam has been unfairly criticized and ridiculed in the west for centuries. *Al Jazeera English*. Retrieved from http://www.aljazeera.com/indepth/opinion/2015/01/charlie-hebdo-twilight-western–201511063740106115.html

Al Jazeera English. (14 January 2015). Tribute paid to slain French Muslim policeman. *Al Jazeera English*. Retrieved from http://www.aljazeera.com/video/europe/2015/01/tribute-paid-slain-french-muslim-policeman-2015113215020146152.html

Al Jazeera English. (19 January 2015). Anti-*Charlie Hebdo* protest held in Chechnya. *Al Jazeera English*. Retrieved from http://www.aljazeera.com/news/europe/2015/01/anti-charlie-hebdo-protest-held-chechnya-201511910042173574.html

Alderman, L., & Bilefsky, D. (11 January 2015). Huge Show of Solidarity in Paris against Terrorism. *The New York Times*. Retrieved from https://www.nytimes.com/2015/01/12/world/europe/paris-march-against-terror-charlie-hebdo.html

Alexander, H. (11 January 2015). Funeral for French policeman Ahmed Merabet held in Paris. *The Telegraph* Retrieved from http://www.telegraph.co.uk/news/worldnews/europe/france/11338404/Funeral-for-French-policeman-Ahmed-Merabet-held-in-Paris.html

AlSayyad, N. (2001). *Hybrid urbanism: On the identity discourse and the built environment*. Westport, CT: Praeger Publishers.

Altheide, D. L. (1987). Format and symbols in TV coverage of terrorism in the United States and Great Britain. *International Studies Quarterly, 31*(2), 161–176.

Aneja, A. (8 January 2015). Watch how the world reacted to the *Charlie Hebdo* Attack. *Time*. Retrieved from http://time.com/3660809/charlie-hebdo-paris-reactions/

Archetti, C. (2012). *Understanding terrorism in the age of global media: A communication approach*. Basingstoke: Palgrave Macmillan.

Bacchi, U. (23 January 2015). Paris shooting: Jihadi murderer Amedy Coulibaly given secret burial in Paris unmarked grave. *The International Business Times*. Retrieved from http://www.ibtimes.co.uk/paris-shooting-jihadi-murderer-amedy-coulibaly-given-secret-burial-paris-unmarked-grave-1484857

Back, L. (2007). *The art of listening*. London: Bloomsbury.

Badiou, A. (2015). *Being and event*. London: Continuum.

Badouard, R. (2016). Beyond 'points of control': Logics of digital governmentality. *Internet Policy Review*, 5(3), 1–11.

Baker, L., & Heneghan, T. (12 January 2015). Netanyahu out of step with French leaders at Paris rally. *Reuters*. Retrieved from http://www.reuters.com/article/us-france-shooting-netanyahu/netanyahu-out-of-step-with-french-leaders-at-paris-rally-idUSKBN0KL16P20150112

BBC News. (12 July 2005). 'Not afraid' website overwhelmed. *BBC News*. Retrieved from http://news.bbc.co.uk/2/hi/uk_news/england/london/4674425.stm

BBC News. (10 January 2015). *Charlie Hebdo* attack: Ahmed Merabet's family speak out. *BBC News*. Retrieved from http://www.bbc.com/news/world-europe-30761229

BBC News. (13 January 2015). France attacks: War with terrorism not Islam, PM Valls says. *BBC News*. Retrieved from http://www.bbc.com/news/world-europe-30794973

BBC News. (13 October 2016). Paris attacks: 'Coulibaly given orders by email'. *BBC News*. Retrieved from http://www.bbc.com/news/world-europe-34514244

BBC News. (18 August 2015). *Paris shootings survivor sues French media*. Retrieved from http://www.bbc.com/news/world-europe-33983599

BBC News. (28 August 2015). *Did French media put lives at risk?* Retrieved from http://www.bbc.com/news/world-europe-34071842

Bennett, W. L., & Segerberg, A. (2012). The logic of connective action. *Information, Communication & Society*, 15(5), 739–768.

Bentley, P. (8 January 2015). 'He died defending the right to ridicule his faith': France unites behind #JeSuisAhmed on Twitter in tribute to Muslim officer slain by fanatics as he begged for his life. *Daily Mail*. Retrieved from http://www.dailymail.co.uk/news/article-2901681/Hero-police-officer-executed-street-married-42-year-old-Muslim-assigned-patrol-Paris-neighbourhood-Charlie-Hebdo-offices-located.html

BFM TV. (13 January 2015). Hommage aux policiers tués: les larmes retenues de Manuel Valls. *BFM TV*. Retrieved from http://www.bfmtv.com/politique/hommage-aux-policiers-tues-les-larmes-retenues-de-manuel-valls-857129.html

Bilefsky, D., & de la Baume, M. (10 January 2015). French Premier declares 'war' on Radical Islam as Paris girds for rally. *The New York Times*. Retrieved from https://www.nytimes.com/2015/01/11/world/europe/paris-terrorist-attacks.html.

Billis, D. (Ed.) (2010). *Hybrid organizations and the third sector: Challenges for practice, theory and policy*. Houndmills: Palgrave Macmillan.

Borchgrevink, A. (2013). *A Norwegian tragedy: Anders Behring Breivik and the Massacre on Utøya*. Cambridge: Polity Press.

Boumans, J. W., & Trilling, D. (2016). Taking stock of the toolkit: An overview of relevant automated content analysis approaches and techniques for digital journalism scholars. *Digital Journalism*, 4(1), 8–23.

Breed, A. (8 January 2015). Alongside 'Je Suis Charlie', slain officer inspires his own social media refrain. *The New York Times*. Retrieved from https://www.nytimes.com/2015/01/09/world/europe/charlie-hebdo-terror-attack-je-suis-ahmed-merabet.html

Brenner, M. (August, 2015). The troubling question in the French Jewish community: Is it time to leave? *Vanity Fair*. Retrieved from https://www.vanityfair.com/news/2015/07/anti-semitism-france-hostage-hyper-cacher-kosher-market

Brown, W. (2009). Introduction. In T. Asad, W. Brown, J. Butler, & S. Mahmood (Eds.), *Is critique secular? Blashemy, injury and free speech* (pp. 7–19). Berkeley, CA: University of California Press.

Bruno, N. (2011). *Tweet first, verify later? How real-time information is changing the coverage of worldwide crisis events*. Reuters Institute for the Study of Journalism, University of Oxford, Oxford.

Burke, J. (8 January 2015). Paris attack suspect Chérif Kouachi had been jailed for terror offences. *The Guardian*. Retrieved from https://www.theguardian.com/world/2015/jan/08/paris-attack-suspect-cherif-kouchi-jailed-terror-offences-2008-charlie-hebdo

Butler, J. (2004). *Precarious life: The power of mourning and violence*. London: Verso.

Castells, M. (2009). *Communication power*. Oxford: Oxford University Press.

Chadwick, A. (2013). *The hybrid media system: Politics and power*. Oxford: Oxford University Press.

Chisafis, A. (12 January 2015). *Charlie Hebdo* attackers: Born, raised and radicalized in Paris. *The Guardian*. Retrieved from https://www.theguardian.com/world/2015/jan/12/-sp-charlie-hebdo-attackers-kids-france-radicalised-paris

CNN. (7 January 2015). 'Je suis Charlie': Paris gathers after terror attack. *CNN*. Retrieved from https://www.youtube.com/watch?v=vWkdmLH7xdE

CNN. (11 January 2015). *Gunman tried to justify market raid to hostages, recording apparently shows*. Retrieved from https://edition.cnn.com/2015/01/10/world/france-market-shooting-scene/index.html

CNN. (31 January 2015). *Official: Gunman recorded terror attack on Parisian kosher grocery*. Retrieved from https://edition.cnn.com/2015/01/30/europe/coulibaly-kosher-grocery-attack/index.html

Coleman, S., & Elsner, J. (1998). Performing pilgrimage: Walsingham and the ritual constructions of irony. In F. Hughes-Freeland (Ed.), *Ritual, performance, media*. London: Routledge.

Cottle, S. (2006a). Mediatized rituals: Beyond manufacturing consent. *Media, Culture & Society*, *28*(3), 411–432.

Cottle, S. (2006b). *Mediatized conflict: Developments in media and conflict studies*. Maidenhead: Open University Press.

Cottle, S. (2014). Rethinking media and disasters in a globalage: What's changed and why it matters. *Media, War & Conflict*, *7*(1), 3–22.

Couldry, N. (2003). *Media rituals: A critical approach*. London: Routledge.

Couldry, N. (2012). *Media, society, world: Social theory and digital media practice*. Cambridge: Polity Press.

Couldry, N., & Hepp, A. (2016). *The mediated construction of reality*. Cambridge: Polity Press.

Couldry, N., & Hepp, A. (2017). The continuing lure of the mediated centre in times of deep mediatization: Media events and its enduring legacy. *Media, Culture & Society*, first published August 18, 2017.

Daily Mail. (10 January 2015). Killers burst in, the boss said 'Hide!'... then bluffed his way free: He made them COFFEE, then ran for his life. Retrieved from http://www.dailymail.co.uk/news/article-2904581/Owner-printers-held-hostage-dramatic-siege-Kouachi-brothers-dressed-terrorists-wounds-COFFEE-reveals-insists-s-sorry-died.html

Davenport, T. H., & Beck, J. C. (2001). *The attention economy: Understanding the new currency of business*. Boston, MA: Harvard Business School Press.

Dawes, S. (2017). #JeSuisCharlie, #JeNeSuisPasCharlie and Ad Hoc Publics. In G. Titley, D. Freedman, G. Khiabany, & A. Mondon (Eds.), *After Charlie Hebdo: Terror, racism and free speech* (pp. 180–191). London: Zed Books.

Dayan, D. (2006). *La terreur spectacle. Terrorisme et télévision*. Bruxelles: De Boeck.

Dayan, D. (2010). Beyond media events: Disenchantment, derailment, disruption. In N. Couldry, A. Hepp, & F. Krotz (Eds.), *Media events in a global age* (pp. 23–31). Abingdon: Routledge.

Dayan, D., & Katz, E. (1992). *Media events: The live broadcasting of history*. Cambridge, MA: Harvard University Press.

De la Baume, M., & Bilefsky, D. (15 January 2015). Bodies of French Gunmen Lie Unburied, and, It Appears, Mostly Unwanted. *The New York Times*. Retrieved from https://www.nytimes.com/2015/01/16/world/europe/bodies-of-french-gunmen-lie-unburied-and-largely-unwanted.html?mcubz=3

De Mareschal, E. (13 January 2015). Musulmans, juifs et policiers pleurent Ahmed Merabet. *Le Figaro*. Retrieved from http://www.lefigaro.fr/actualite-france/2015/01/13/01016-20150113ARTFIG00418-musulmans-juifs-et-policiers-pleurent-ahmed-merabet.php

De Royer, S. (10 January 2015). Hollande appelle à « se lever » contre le terrorisme. *Le Figaro*. Retrieved from http://www.lefigaro.fr/politique/2015/01/09/01002-20150109ARTFIG00331-dans-la-crise-hollande-se-veut-le-garant-de-l-unite.php

Dearden, L. (12 January 2015). Paris attacks: Hamas condemns *Charlie Hebdo* massacre after Netanyahu makes comparison to Gaza rockets. *The Independent*. Retrieved from http://www.independent.co.uk/news/world/europe/paris-attacks-hamas-condemns-charlie-hebdo-massacre-after-netanyahu-makes-comparison-to-gaza-rockets-9970096.html

Deleuze, G. (1994). *Difference and repetition*. London: Athlone Press.

Devichand, M. (3 January 2016). How the world was changed by the slogan 'Je Suis Charlie'. *BBC News*. Retrieved from http://www.bbc.com/news/blogs-trending-35108339

Dias, E. (15 January 2015). Pope Francis speaks out on *Charlie Hebdo*: 'One Cannot Make Fun of Faith'. *Time*. Retrieved from http://time.com/3668875/pope-francis-charlie-hebdo/

Eade, J., & Sallinow, M. J. (Eds.). (1999). *Contesting the sacred: The anthropology of Christian pilgrimage*. London: Routledge.

Ehrhard, V., & Garrier, N. (2015). Communication techniques – The Paris terrorist attacks, January 2015. *Nordic Crisis Communication Conference*, 27 October 2015, Helsinki.

Eide, E., Kunelius, R., & Phillips, A. (Eds.). (2008). *Transnational media events: The Mohammed Cartoons and the imagined clash of civilizations.* Gothenburg: Nordicom.

Eskjær, M., Hjarvard, S., & Mortensen, M. (Eds.). (2015). *The dynamics of mediatized conflicts.* New York, NY: Peter Lang.

Faraj, S., & Azad, B. (2012). The materiality of technology: An affordance perspective. In P. M. Leonardi, B. Nardi, & J. Kallinikos (Eds.), *Materiality and organizing: Social interaction in a technological world* (pp. 237–258). Oxford: Oxford University Press.

Financial Times. (13 January 2015). Manuel Valls calls for a tougher action against terror. *Financial Times.* Retrieved from https://www.ft.com/content/49760ad6-9b47-11e4-950f-00144feabdc0

Fiske, J. (1994). *Media matters: Everyday culture and political change.* Minneapolis, MN: University of Minnesota Press.

France Diplomatique. (7 January 2015). *Speech of President Hollande. France Diplomatique.* Retrieved from http://www.diplomatie.gouv.fr/en/the-ministry-and-its-network/events/article/attackagainst-charlie-hebdo

Frosh, P., & Pinchevski, A. (2009). *Media witnessing: Testimony in the age of mass communication.* Basingstoke: Palgrave Macmillan.

Gayle, E. (13 January 2015). *Charlie Hebdo*: Israeli paper deletes women from Paris march. *Euronews.* Retrieved from http://www.euronews.com/2015/01/13/charlie-hebdo-israeli-paper-deletes-women-from-paris-march-photo

Gibson, J. J. (1979). *The ecological approach to visual perception.* Boston, MA: Houghton Mifflin.

Giglietto, F., & Lee, Y. (2015). 'To be or not to be Charlie: Twitter hashtags as a discourse and counterdiscourse in the aftermath of the 2015 *Charlie Hebdo* shooting in France'. *Workshop on Making Sense of Microposts at the 24th International World Wide Web Conference.*

Girginova, K. (2015). New media, creativity, and the olympics: A case study into the use of #NBCFail during the sochi winter games. *Communication & Sport, 4*(3), 243–260.

Goldhaber, M. H. (1997). The attention economy and the net. *First Monday, 2*(4).

Goyette, B. (10 January 2015). French Prime Minister Manuel Valls: We are at war against terrorism and radical Islam. *The Huffington Post.* Retrieved from https://www.huffingtonpost.com/2015/01/10/manuel-valls-radical-islam_n_6449414.html

Graham-Harrison, E. (10 January 2015). Paris policeman's brother: 'Islam is a religion of love. My brother was killed by terrorists, by false Muslims'. *The Guardian.* Retrieved from https://www.theguardian.com/world/2015/jan/10/charlie-hebdo-policeman-murder-ahmed-merabet

Greer, C. (2004). Crime, media and community: Grief and virtual engagement in late modernity. In J. Ferrell, K. Hayward, W. Morrison, & M. Presdee (Eds.), *Cultural criminology unleashed* (pp. 109–118). London: Glasshouse Press.

The Guardian. (8 February 2015). British Muslims gather in London to protest against Muhammad cartoons. *The Guardian.* Retrieved from https://www.theguardian.com/world/2015/feb/08/british-muslims-london-protest-against-muhammad-cartoon-charlie-hebdo

The Guardian. (11 January 2015). *Paris supermarket attacker claims allegiance to Islamic State in video.* Retrieved from https://www.theguardian.com/world/2015/jan/11/paris-supermarket-attacker-islamic-state-video-isis-amedy-coulibaly

The Guardian. (19 August 2015). *Charlie Hebdo hostage sues French media for putting his life on danger.* Retrieved from https://www.theguardian.com/world/2015/aug/19/charlie-hebdo-hostage-sues-french-media-for-putting-his-life-in-danger

Hassan, R. (2009). *Empires of speed: Time and acceleration of politics and society.* Leiden: Brill.

Heikka, T., Valaskivi, K., & Uskali, T. (2016). Crashing a national media event: Circulation of social imaginaries in the Gatecrashers Riots in Finland. In B. Miltu & S. Poulakidakos (Eds.), *Media events: A critical contemporary approach* (pp. 92–113). Basingstoke: Palgrave Macmillan.

Hepp, A. (2015). *Transcultural communication.* Malden, MA: Wiley-Blackwell.

Hepp, A., & Couldry, N. (2010). Introduction: Media events in globalized media cultures. In N. Couldry, A. Hepp, & F. Krotz (Eds.), *Media events in a global age* (pp. 1–20). Abingdon: Routledge.

Hepp, A., & Krotz, F. (2008). Media events, globalization and cultural change: An introduction to the special issue. *Communications. The European Journal of Communication Research, 33*(3), 265–272.

Hervik, P. (2008). The original spin and its side effects: Freedom of speech as Danish News management. In E. Eide, R. Kunelius, & A. Phillips (Eds.), *Transnational media events: The Mohammed Cartoons and the imagined clash of civilizations.* (pp. 59–80). Gothenburh: Nordicom.

Hervik, P. (2018). Ten years after the Danish Muhammad Cartoon News Stories: Terror and radicalization as predictable media events. *Television & New Media, 19*(2), 146–154.

Hervik, P., Eide, E., & Kunelius, R. (2008). A long and messy event. In E. Eide, R. Kunelius, & A. Phillips (Eds.), *Transnational media events: The Mohammed Cartoons and the imagined clash of civilizations* (pp. 29–38). Gothenburg: Nordicom.

Hjarvard, S., Mortensen, M., & Eskjær, M. F. (2015). Introduction. Dynamics of mediatized conflicts. In M. F. Eskjær, S. Hjarvard, & M. Mortensen (Eds.), *The dynamics of mediatized conflicts* (pp. 1–27). New York, NY: Peter Lang.

Hokka, J., Valaskivi, K., Sumiala, J., & Laakso, S. (2013). Suomalaiset sanomalehdet uskonnollisen maiseman tuottajina: uskontojournalismi Helsingin Sanomissa, Ilkassa, Kalevassa ja Karjalaisessa vuosina 2007–2011. *Media & Viestintä. Kulttuurin ja yhteiskunnan tutkimuksen lehti, 36*, 6–21.

Huffington Post France. (9 January 2015). Jean-Marie Le Pel appelle à voter Front National et déclare 'Je suis Charlie Martel' après l'attentat de *Charlie Hebdo. Huffington Post France.* Retrieved from http://www.huffingtonpost.fr/2015/01/09/jean-marie-le-pen-front-national-charlie-martel-hebdo-tweet-declarations_n_6443248.html

The Huffington Post. (13 January 2015). *Hidden under a sink, Lilian Lepère had a very close call with the Charlie Hebdo gunmen.* Retrieved from https://www.huffingtonpost.com/2015/01/13/lilian-lepere-charlie-hebdo_n_6465872.html

Huyssen, A. (2000). Present pasts: Media, politics, amnesia. *Public Culture*, *12*(1), 21–38.

Jackson, S. J., & Foucault Welles, B. (2015). Hijacking #myNYPD: Social media dissent and networked counterpublics. *Journal of Communication*, *65*(6), 932–952.

JDD. (15 January 2015). *Charlie Hebdo*: 57% des Français veulent des caricatures mais… *Le Journal Du Dimanche*. Retrieved from http://www.lejdd.fr/Politique/ Sondage-JDD-57-des-Francais-veulent-des-caricatures-mais-713532

Katz, E., & Liebes, T. (2007). 'No More Peace!' How disaster, terror and war have upstaged media events. *International Journal of Communication*, *1*, 157–166.

Katz, E., & Liebes, T. (2010). 'No More Peace!' How disaster, terror and war have upstaged media events. In N. Couldry, A. Hepp, & F. Krotz (Eds.), *Media events in a global age*. Abingdon: Routledge.

Kavoori, A. P., & Fraley, T. (2006). *Media, terrorism, and theory: A reader.* Landam, MD: Rowman & Littlefield.

Kellner, D. (2003). *Media spectacle*. London: Routledge.

Kepel, G. (2017). *Terror in France: The rise of Jihad in the West.* Princeton, NJ: Princeton University Press.

Khiabany, G., & Williamson, M. (2012). Terror, culture and anti-Muslim Rasicm. In D. Freedman & D. Thussu (Eds.), *Media and terrorism: Global perspectives.* London: Sage.

Kicker. (8 January 2015). 5 reasons why the *Charlie Hebdo* massacre in france matters to everyone in the freeworld. *Kicker*. Retrieved from http://gokicker.com/ about/

Klopfenstein, B. (2007). Terrorism and the exploitation of new media. In A. P. Kavoori & T. Fraley (Eds.), *Media, terrorism and theory: A reader* (pp. 107–120). Lanham, MD: Rowman & Littlefield.

Kraidy, M. M. (2005). *Hybridity, or the cultural logic of globalization*. Philadelphia, PA: Temple University Press.

Kraidy, M. M., & Mourad, S. (2010). Hypermedia space and global communication studies: Lessons from the Middle East. *Global Media Journal*, *8*(16), Article No. 8.

Kreiss, D., Meadows, L., & Remensperger, J. (2014). Political performance, boundary spaces, and active spectatorship: Media production at the 2012 Democratic National Convention. *Journalism*, *16*(5), 577–595.

Kunelius, R., & Nossek, H. (2008). Between the ritual and the rational. From media events to moments of global public spheres? In E. Eide, R. Kunelius, & A. Phillips (Eds.), *Transnational media events: The Mohammed Cartoons and the imagined clash of civilizations* (pp. 253–274). Gothenburg: Nordicom.

Kyriakidou, M. (2008). Rethinking media events in the context of a global public sphere: Exploring the audience of global disasters in Greece. *Communications. The European Journal of Communication Research*, *33*(3), 273–291.

Lallement, P. (23 January 2015). L'itinéraire exemplaire d'Ahmed Merabet. *Paris Match*. Retrieved from http://www.parismatch.com/Actu/Societe/Son-itineraire- exemplaire-Ahmed-Merabet-695190

Latour, B. (1993). *We have never been modern* (C. Porter, Trans.). Cambridge, MA: Harvard University Press.

Latour, B. (2005). *Reassembling the social: An introduction to actor-network-theory.* Oxford: Oxford University Press.

Lazard, V., & Le Bailly, D. (26 January 2015). 'Levez-vous où j'vais vous allumer': la vidéo macabre de l'Hyper Cacher. *Le Nouvel Observateur.* Retrieved from http://tempsreel.nouvelobs.com/charlie-hebdo/20150225.OBS3345/levez-vous-ou-j-vais-vous-allumer-la-video-macabre-de-l-hyper-cacher.html

Le Monde. (8 January 2015a). L'immense emotion de Patrick Pelloux, urgentiste et chroniqueur à '*Charlie Hebdo*'. *Le Monde.* Retrieved from http://www.lemonde.fr/actualite-medias/video/2015/01/08/charlie-hebdo-l-emotion-de-patrick-pelloux-urgentiste-et-chroniqueur_4551679_3236.html

Le Monde. (8 January 2015b). Hommage mondial pour '*Charlie Hebdo*'. *Le Monde.* Retrieved from http://www.lemonde.fr/attaque-contre-charlie-hebdo/video/2015/01/08/hommage-mondial-pour-charlie-hebdo_4551263_4550668.html

Le Monde. (8 January 2016). Les ex-otages de l'Hyper Cacher retirent leur plainte contre BFM. *Le Monde.* Retrieved from http://www.lemonde.fr/police-justice/article/2016/01/08/hyper-cacher-les-otages-de-la-chambre-froide-retirent-leur-plainte-contre-bfm-tv_4844031_1653578.html

Le Parisien. (11 January 2015). François Hollande rend visite à la famille du policier Ahmed Merabet. *Le Parisien.* Retrieved from http://www.leparisien.fr/livry-gargan-93190/francois-hollande-rend-visite-a-la-famille-du-policier-ahmed-merabet-11-01-2015-4437653.php

Lee, B., & LiPuma, E. (2002). Cultures of circulation: The imaginations of modernity. *Public Culture, 14*(1), 191–213.

Lepère, L. (12 January 2015). Rescapé des frères Kouachi interview France 2. *France 2.* Retrieved from https://www.youtube.com/watch?time_continue=1&v=w5Psw056JEw

Libération. (2015). «*Charlie Hebdo*»: un hommage mondial. *Libération.* Retrieved from http://www.liberation.fr/video/2015/01/08/charlie-hebdo-un-hommage-mondial_1176339

Lichfield, J. (11 January 2015). Paris march: Global leaders join 'unprecedented' rally in largest demonstration in history of France. *The Independent.* Retrieved from http://www.independent.co.uk/news/world/europe/world-leaders-gather-for-freedom-march-in-paris-as-million-expected-at-rally-9970512.html

Liebes, T. (1997). *Reporting the Arab–Israeli conflict: How hegemony works.* London: Routledge.

Liebes, T. (1998). Television's disaster marathons. A danger for democratic processes? In T. Liebes & J. Curran (Eds.), *Media, ritual and identity* (pp. 71–84). London: Routledge.

Liebes, T., & Blondheim, M. (2005). Myths to the rescue: How live television intervenes in history. In E. W. Rothenbuhler & M. Coman (Eds.), *Media anthropology* (pp. 188–198). Thousand Oaks, CA: Sage.

Line, H. (13 January 2015). Jewish victims of Paris shootings mourned at Israeli funeral. *The Telegraph.* Retrieved from http://www.telegraph.co.uk/news/

worldnews/middleeast/israel/11342184/Jewish-victims-of-Paris-shootings-mourned-at-Israeli-funeral.html

Linshi, J. (11 January 2015). Man who filmed terrorists shooting Paris cop says he regrets sharing video. *Time*. Retrieved from http://time.com/3662914/paris-attack-video/

Linshi, J. (18 January 2015). 42% of French opposed to *Charlie Hebdo*'s Cartoons of the Prophet Muhammad, poll finds. *Time*. Retrieved from http://time.com/3672921/charlie-hebdo-prophet-muhammad-muslim-cartoon-poll/

Mapping Media Freedom. (21 August 2015). *Lawsuit takes French media to task for Charlie Hebdo reporting*. Retrieved from https://mappingmediafreedom.org/plus/index.php/2015/08/21/lawsuit-takes-french-media-to-task-for-charlie-hebdo-reporting

Marlière, P. (2017). The meaning of 'Charlie': The debate on the troubled French identity. In G. Titley, D. Freedman, G. Khiabany, & A. Mondon (Eds.), *After Charlie Hebdo: Terror, racism and free speech* (pp. 46–62). London: Zed Books.

Messina, C. (2007). Groups for Twitter; or A Proposal for Twitter Tag Channels. *Factory Joe*. Retrieved from https://factoryjoe.com/2007/08/25/groups-for-twitter-or-a-proposal-for-twitter-tag-channels/

Morris, N. (7 January 2015). *Charlie Hebdo* attack: World leaders unite in condemning 'barbaric' Paris killings. *The Independent*. Retrieved from http://www.independent.co.uk/news/world/europe/charlie-hebdo-attack-world-leaders-condemn-barbaric-killings-9963622.html

Muhammad, H. (8 January 2015). French Muslims fear surge of Islamophobia after *Charlie Hebdo* attack. *Al Jazeera America*. Retrieved from http://america.aljazeera.com/articles/2015/1/8/in muslim-neighborhoodsinparisgriefandfear.html

Mullin, G., & Boyle, D. (8 January 2015). Paris goes dark for *Charlie Hebdo*: Eiffel Tower's lights are turned off as vigils are held around globe for 12 victims slaughtered by fanatics. *Daily Mail*. Retrieved from http://www.dailymail.co.uk/news/article-2902025/France-comes-standstill-remember-Charlie-Hebdo-victims-people-worldwide-join-poignant-vigil.html

Murthy, D. (2012). Towards sociological understanding of social media: Theorizing Twitter. *Sociology*, *46*(6), 1059–1073.

Muschert, G., & Sumiala, J. (Eds.). (2012). *School shootings: Mediatized violence in a global age*. Bingley: Emerald Group Publishing.

Nacos, B. (2016). *Mass-mediated terrorism: Mainstream and digital media in terrorism and counterterrorism*. Lanham: Rowman and Littlefield Publishers.

NBC. (13 January 2015). *Charlie Hebdo* Attack: Pakistan Cleric Holds Funerals for Kouachi Brothers. *NBC*. Retrieved from https://www.nbcnews.com/storyline/paris-magazine-attack/charlie-hebdo-attack-pakistan-cleric-holds-funerals-kouachi-brothers-n285011

Nianias, H. (12 January 2015). 'Israel is your home' Benjamin Netanyahu tells French Jews after *Charlie Hebdo* rally. *The Independent*. Retrieved from http://www.independent.co.uk/news/people/israel-is-your-home-benjamin-netanyahu-tells-french-jews-after-charlie-hebdo-rally-9971954.html

Nossek, H. (2008). 'News media' – Media events: Terrorist acts as media events. *Communications. The Journal of European Communication Research, 33*(3), 313–330.

Pandell, L. (19 May 2017). An oral history of the #Hashtag. *Wired*. Retrieved from https://www.wired.com/2017/05/oral-history-hashtag/

Papacharissi, Z. (2015). *Affective publics: Sentiment, technology, and politics*. Oxford: Oxford University Press.

Parfitt, T. (19 January 2015). Chechnya holds mass rally against *Charlie Hebdo* 'Prophet Mohammed' Cartoons. *The Telegraph*. Retrieved from http://www.telegraph.co.uk/news/worldnews/europe/russia/11355233/Chechnya-holds-mass-rally-against-Charlie-Hebdo-Prophet-Mohammed-cartoons.html

Pariser, E. (2011). *The filter bubble: What the Internet is hiding from you*. London, UK: Penguin Books.

Pelletier, E. (30 January 2015). Coulibaly a envoyé les images depuis l'Hyper Cacher. *L'Express*. Retrieved from http://www.lexpress.fr/actualite/societe/enquete/coulibaly-a-envoye-les-images-de-la-tuerie-de-l-hyper-cacher_1646812.html

Penketh, A. (8 January 2015). Policeman Ahmed Merabet mourned after death in *Charlie Hebdo* attack. *The Guardian*. Retrieved from https://www.theguardian.com/world/2015/jan/08/ahmed-merabet-mourned-charlie-hebdo-paris-attack

Peterson, M. A. (2005). *Anthropology and mass communication: Media and myth in the new millennium*. Oxford: Berghahn Books.

Potet, F. (9 January 2015). «Je suis Charlie», c'est lui. *Le Monde*. Retrieved from http://www.lemonde.fr/m-actu/article/2015/01/09/je-suis-charlie-c-est-lui_4552523_4497186.html

Procter, R., Vis, F., & Voss, A. (2013). Reading the riots on Twitter: Methodological innovation for the analysis of big data. *International Journal of Social Research Methodology, 16*(3), 197–214.

Raittila, P., Koljonen, K., & Väliverronen, J. (2010). *Journalism and school shootings in Finland 2007–2008*. Tampere: Tampere University Press.

Rehman, I. (2016). The Sword and the Swastika: How a medieval warlord became a fascist icon. *War on the Rocks*. Retrieved from https://warontherocks.com/2016/11/the-sword-and-the-swastika-how-a-medieval-warlord-became-a-fascist-icon/

Relph, S. (15 January 2015). *Charlie Hebdo* funerals: 'Guardian angel' cartoonists 'dreams of freedom will live on'. *Daily Mirror*. Retrieved from http://www.mirror.co.uk/news/world-news/charlie-hebdo-funerals-guardian-angel-4987381

RFI. (13 February 2015). *French broadcasters protest at official criticism of Charlie Hebdo coverage*. Retrieved from http://en.rfi.fr/culture/20150213-french-broadcasters-protest-official-criticism-charlie-hebdo-coverage

Rothenbuhler, E. W. (1998). *Ritual communication: From everyday conversation to mediated ceremony*. Thousand Oaks, CA: Sage.

Rothenbuhler, E. W. (2010). Media events in the age of terrorism and Internet. *The Romanian Review of Journalism and Communication, IV*(2), 34–41.

Rothenbuhler, E. W., & Coman, M. (2005). *Media anthropology*. Thousand Oaks, CA: Sage.

Roy, O. (2016). *Jihad and death: The global appeal of Islamic State*. London: Hurst & Company.

Sabin, L. (3 April 2015). Paris kosher supermarket massacre: French TV channel BFM sued by victims' families over coverage that allegedly put 'lives of hostages in danger'. *The Independent.* Retrieved from http://www.independent.co.uk/news/world/europe/french-tv-channel-bfm-sued-over-coverage-of-paris-kosher-supermarket-massacre-that-allegedly-put-10154185.html

Said, E. (1981/1997). *Covering Islam: How the media and the experts determine how we see the rest of the world.* London: Vintage Books.

Samuel, H. (15 January 2015). *Charlie Hebdo* cartoonist funerals held in Paris as million more copies sell out. *The Telegraph.* Retrieved from http://www.telegraph.co.uk/news/worldnews/europe/france/11348620/Charlie-Hebdo-cartoonist-funerals-held-in-Paris-as-million-more-copies-sell-out.html

Satter, R. (11 January 2015). AP exclusive: Witness to Paris officer's death regrets video. *Associated Press.* Retrieved from https://www.apnews.com/5e1ee93021b941629186882f03f1bb79

Saul, S. (8 January 2015). *Charlie Hebdo* shooting: Far-right Front National leader Marine Le Pen 'wants to offer France referendum on the death penalty. *The Independent.* Retrieved from http://www.independent.co.uk/news/world/europe/charlie-hebdo-shooting-far-right-front-national-leader-marine-le-pen-wants-to-offer-france-9965607.html

Scannell, P. (1995). Media events (Review). *Media, Culture & Society, 17*(1), 151–157.

Scannell, P. (2001). Editorial. *Media, Culture & Society, 12*(6), 699–705.

Scannell, P. (2014). *Television and the meaning of 'Live': An enquiry into the human situation.* Cambridge: Polity Press.

Scannell, P. (2017). Media events: An afterword. *Media, Culture & Society, 40*(1), 153–157.

Schechter, A. (12 January 2015). Netanyahu's Paris Appearance Was a PR Disaster. *Haaretz.* http://www.haaretz.com/israel-news/.premium-1.636737

Scott, K. (2015). The pragmatics of hashtags: Inference and conversational style on Twitter. *Journal of Pragmatics, 81*, 8–20.

Selby, J. (8 January 2015). Banksy's illustrated response to the *Charlie Hebdo* attack isn't by Banksy. But it is striking. *The Independent.* Retrieved from http://www.independent.co.uk/news/people/banksys-striking-illustrated-response-to-the-charlie-hebdo-attack-9964198.html

Sewell, W. H. (2005). *Logics of history: Social theory and social transformation.* Chicago, IL: University of Chicago Press.

Silverstone, R. (2007). *Media and morality: On the rise of the Mediapolis.* Cambridge: Polity.

Smith, K., & Leavy, P. (Eds.). (2009). *Hybrid identities: Theoretical and empirical examinations.* London: Haymarket Books.

Sonnevend, J. (2016). *Stories without borders: The Berlin wall and the making of a global iconic event.* New York, NY: Oxford University Press.

Sputnik International. (3 April 2015). *Too much info? Hostages of Paris attack sue media over location reports.* Retrieved from https://sputniknews.com/europe/201504031020421891/

Sreberny, A. (2016). The 2015 *Charlie Hebdo*: Killings, media event chains, and global political responses. *International Journal of Communication*, *10*, 3485–3502.

Stoffregen, T. A. (2003). Affordances as properties of the animal-environment system. *Ecological Psychology*, *15*(2), 115–134.

Sulzer, A. (10 January 2015). Les réseaux sociaux servent-ils à faire l'apologie des attentats? *L'Express*. Retrieved from http://www.lexpress.fr/actualite/societe/les-reseaux-sociaux-servent-ils-a-faire-l-apologie-des-attentats_1639336.html

Sumiala, J. (2008). Circulation. In D. Morgan (Ed.), *Keywords in religion, media, and culture* (pp. 44–55). London: Routledge.

Sumiala, J. (2013). *Media and ritual: Death, community and everyday life*. London: Routledge.

Sumiala, J. (2014). Mediatized ritual: Expanding the field in the study of media and ritual. *Sociology Compass*, *8*(7), 939–947.

Sumiala, J. (2017). 'Je suis Charlie' and the digital mediascape: The politics of death in the *Charlie Hebdo* mourning rituals. *Journal of Ethnology and Folkloristics*, *11*(1), 111–126.

Sumiala, J., & Tikka, M. (2011). Imagining globalized fears: School shooting videos and circulation of violence on YouTube. *Social Anthropology*, *19*(3), 254–267.

Sumiala, J., & Tikka, M. (2013). Broadcast yourself – Global news! A netnography of the 'Flotilla' News on YouTube. *Communication, Culture and Critique*, *6*(2), 201–352.

Sumiala, J., Tikka, M., Huhtamäki, J., & Valaskivi, K. (2016). #JeSuisCharlie: Towards a multi-method study of hybrid media events. *Media and Communication*, *4*(4), 97–108.

Sumiala, J., Tikka, M., & Valaskivi, K. (forthcoming). *Charlie Hebdo*, 2015 – 'Liveness' and acceleration of conflict in a hybrid media event. *Media, War & Conflict*.

Sumiala, J., & Valaskivi, K. (2018). Introduction. Towards hybrid media events of terrorist violence. *Television & New Media*, *19*(2), 128–135. Special issue Terror as a Media Event, guest edited by J. Sumiala & K. Valaskivi, Autumn.

Tchernookova, A. (16 January 2015). Russia's reaction to the '*Charlie Hebdo*' attacks and what it says about Putin. *Vice News*. Retrieved from https://news.vice.com/article/russias-reaction-to-the-charlie-hebdo-attacks-and-what-it-says-about-putin

The Commentator. (11 January 2015). Shame of Palestinian leader at *Charlie Hebdo* demo. *The Commentator*. Retrieved from http://www.thecommentator.com/article/5523/shame_of_palestinian_leader_at_charlie_hebdo_demo

The Independent. (10 January 2015). *Paris attackers interview with French TV station: 'We are defenders of the Prophet… We took vengeance', said Charlie Hebdo killer Cherif Kouachi*. Retrieved from http://www.independent.co.uk/news/world/europe/paris-attackers-gave-interview-to-french-tv-station-we-are-defenders-of-the-prophet-we-took-9969749.html

The Independent. (9 January 2015). *Paris shootings: How the sieges with Charlie Hebdo killers at Dammartin-en-Goele print works and Jewish grocer ended*. Retrieved from http://www.independent.co.uk/news/world/europe/paris-shootings-how-sieges-at-dammartin-en-goele-print-works-and-jewish-grocer-ended-9968962.html

The Telegraph. (12 January 2015). Reuters: US media questions why neither Barack Obama nor top US officials attended Paris *Charlie Hebdo* rally. *The Telegraph.* Retrieved from http://www.telegraph.co.uk/news/worldnews/europe/france/ 11339477/US-media-questions-why-neither-Barack-Obama-nor-top-US-officials-attended-Paris-Charlie-Hebdo-rally.html

Therborn, G. (2000). At the birth of second century sociology: Times of reflexivity, spaces of identity, and nodes of knowledge. *British Journal of Sociology, 51*(1), 37–57.

Titley, G. (2017). Introduction: Becoming symbolic: From *Charlie Hebdo* to 'Charlie Hebdo'. In G. Titley, D. Freedman, G. Khiabany, & A. Mondon (Eds.), *After Charlie Hebdo: Terror, racism and free speech* (pp. 1–27). London: Zed Books.

Todd, E. (2015). *Who is Charlie? Xenophobia and the new middle class.* Cambridge, MA: Polity Press.

Urry, J. (2007). *Mobilities.* Cambridge: Polity Press.

Utz, S., Schultz, F., & Glocka, S. (2013). Crisis communication online: How medium, crisis type and emotions affected public reactions in the Fukushima Daiichi Nuclear Disaster. *Public Relations Review, 39*(1), 40–46.

Vaccari, C., Chadwick, A., & O'Loughlin, B. (2015). Dual screening the political: Media events, social media, and citizen engagement. *Journal of Communication, 65*(6), 1041–1061.

Valaskivi, K., & Sumiala, J. (2014). Introduction: Circulating social imaginaries – A theoretical and methodological perspective. *European Journal of Cultural Studies, 17*(3), 229–243.

Van Dijck, J. (2013). *The culture of connectivity: A critical history of social media.* New York, NY: Oxford University Press.

Ventre, D. (2016). *Information warfare.* (2nd ed.). London: Wiley.

Vulliamy, E. (18 January 2015). A week inside *Charlie Hebdo*: How the 'survival issue' was made. *The Guardian.* Retrieved from https://www.theguardian.com/ media/2015/jan/18/charlie-hebdo-we-cant-let-this-change-our-cartoons-nor-will-it

Wagner-Pacifici, R. (2017). *What is an event?* Chicago, IL: University of Chicago Press.

Walt, V. (8 January 2015). Suspects in *Charlie Hebdo* attack evade authorities for a second day. *Time.* Retrieved from http://time.com/3659164/charlie-hebdo-paris-suspects/

Watt, H. (7 January 2015). Marine Le Pen condemns 'murderous ideology' in the aftermath of *Charlie Hebdo* shooting. *The Telegraph.* Retrieved from http:// www.telegraph.co.uk/news/11331595/Marine-Le-Pen-condemns-murderous-ideology-in-the-aftermath-of-Charlie-Hebdo-shooting.html

Webster, J. G. (2014). *The marketplace of attention: How audiences take shape in a digital age.* Cambridge, MA: The MIT Press.

Whatmore, S. (2002). *Hybrid geographies: Natures cultures spaces.* London: Sage.

Whitehead, T. (9 January 2015). Paris *Charlie Hebdo* Attack: Je suis Charlie hashtag one of most popular in Twitter history. *The Telegraph.* Retrieved from http://www.telegraph.co.uk/news/worldnews/europe/france/11336879/

Paris-Charlie-Hebdo-attack-Je-Suis-Charlie-hashtag-one-of-most-popular-in-Twitter-history.html

Willsher, K. (13 January 2015). *Charlie Hebdo* attack: Fallen policeman Ahmed Merabet buried in Bobigny. *The Guardian*. Retrieved from https://www.theguardian.com/world/2015/jan/13/charlie-hebdo-attack-ahmed-merabet-buried-bobigny

Willsher, K., & Quinn, B. (7 January 2015). Solidarity in grief: Thousands attend rallies in wake of *Charlie Hebdo* killings. *The Guardian*. Retrieved from https://www.theguardian.com/world/2015/jan/07/rallies-charlie-hebdo-paris-london-solidarity-grief

Yuhas, A. (29 April 2015). Two dozen writers join *Charlie Hebdo* PEN award protest. *The Guardian*. Retrieved from https://www.theguardian.com/books/2015/apr/29/writers-join-protest-charlie-hebdo-pen-award

Zagato, A. (Ed.). (2015). *The event of Charlie Hebdo. Imaginaries of freedom and control*. New York, NY: Berghahn Books.

Zelizer, B. (2018). Seeing the present, remembering the past: Terror's representations as an excercise in collective memory. *Television & New Media, 19*(2), 136–145.

Index

Acceleration, 17, 20–21, 107
  of circulation, 107–108
  of circulation in hybrid media
    event, 119–121
Accounts, 59–60
Accumulation, 77
  of attention, 87–88
Accuracy, 131, 132
Actor Network Theory (ANT), 7
Actors, 17–18, 57, 126
  accounts and hashtags, 59–60
  anatomy of *Charlie Hebdo*
    attacks on Twitter, 60–72
  hybrid media events
    amplifying, 75–76
  tracing @JeSuisKouachi,
    72–75
Affect(s), 20
  circulating affects, 89–90
  circulation of fear addresses
    diverse audiences, 102–104
  element, 17
  funerals, 96–99
  hybridization and ritual
    practices, 104–105
  Je Suis Charlie' in social media,
    95–96
  mediatized ritualization, 90–91
  narratives opposed to 'Je Suis
    Charlie' solidarity, 99–102
  responses, 89
  rituals intensify sense of
    solidarity in media, 91–95
  role, 104
  violent hybrid media event, 89

Affordance(s), 17–19, 60, 127
  accounts and hashtags, 59–60
  anatomy of *Charlie Hebdo*
    attacks on Twitter, 60–72
  of hashtags, 72–75
  hybrid media events
    amplifying, 75–76
  tracing @JeSuisKouachi,
    72–75
Agency, 17, 57, 59, 70
Ahmed, Sara, 20, 91, 106
After Charlie Hebdo: Terror,
    Racism and Free Speech, 89
Agence France-Presse (AFP), 64
Ahmed Merabet
  death, 77–79
  shooting, 88
Al Jazeera English, 23, 46–47, 85
Al-Qaeda, 111, 129
American internet news service
    Kicker, 1
Amplification, 72
Anglo-American context, 8
Anti-Islam sentiment, 87
Associated Press, 78–79, 82
Attention, 17, 19–20
  accumulation and circulation,
    87–88
  Ahmed Merabet's death,
    77–79
  controversy over video,
    81–83
  economy, 19
  'Je Suis Ahmed' as symbol of
    public solidarity, 83–85

media making Merabet ideal
victim, 80–81
politicizing Muslim body, 86
tracking, 77
Automated content analysis
(ACA), 23, 24
Archetti, Cristina, 132

Bête et Méchant' newspaper,
30–35
BFM TV, 110, 111, 117, 119, 130
broadcast, 114
Twitter user accounts, 116
British Broadcasting Corporation
(BBC), 64
BBC News, 13–14, 37, 41,
81, 86
Buzzfeed, American internet
media company, 64

Cable News Network (CNN),
13–14, 19, 22, 64, 72, 91,
114
Cartoonists' funerals, 98
Catholicism, 30
Ceremonial media events, 13, 96,
98, 123
Ceremoniality, 9–10, 123
Chadwick, Andrew, 6–8, 128, 129
Charlie effect, 86
Charlie Hebdo attacks, 1–5, 23,
24, 29, 35–36, 46, 60, 77,
78, 87, 89–93, 98, 102, 103,
107, 108, 119, 124, 125, 126
anatomy on Twitter, 60–72
circulation connects key
elements, 126–127
and circulation of terrorist
violence, 123
towards discussion of social
and ethical dimensions of

hybrid media events,
127–130
see also 9/11 attacks
Charlie Hebdo media event, 57,
104
hybridization, 87–88
Charlie Hebdo newspaper, 30–35,
46
Charlie Hebdo Twitter account, 65
Charlie Mensuel comics
magazine, 30
Christians, 49, 74, 75
Circulation, 87–88, 126, 127
connecting key elements,
126–127
of representations, 90
Couldry, Nick, 134
Coulibaly, Amedy, 40, 41, 112,
115, 116, 117, 118, 132
'Co-productions' of
broadcasters, 12
Communication, 2–3
ethics, 130, 131
principles, 132
technology, 113
Condensation, 15
counter-narratives challenge
main storyline, 45–49
huge show of solidarity in Paris
against terrorism, 49–51
of meanings, 43
world political elites
demonstrate solidarity,
43–45
Conseil superieur de l'audiovisuel
(CSA), 117
Contemporary media events,
19, 123
Contemporary terrorism, 2–3
Contemporary terrorist
violence, 4

'Contrapuntal', hybridity, 6
Coulibaly's attack, 115
Counter-emotional responses, 93
Counter-narratives, 29
    types, 38
Counternarration, 15
Cultural process, 126

Daily Mail, The, 23, 78, 84, 93,
    108
Daily Mirror, The, 78, 96
Daily Telegraph, The, 78, 87
Dayan, Daniel, 5, 9, 10, 13, 16,
    92, 128
Dammartin-en-Goële, hostage
    situation in, 108−113
Diffusion processes, 13
Digital ethnography, 23, 24,
    25−26, 27, 72
Digital media, 13, 15, 132
    events, 123
    platforms, 20, 90, 98
    remediation in, 35−36
    social norms, 21
    see also Live media
Digital rituals, 90
Disaster marathon, 54, 123
Disenchantment, 12, 13
Disruptive media events, 90, 112,
    123

Emotional/emotions, 20, 89, 91,
    104, 131, 132, 136
    expressions, 104
    reactions, 89
    responses and reactions, 125
Empathy, 89, 112
Empirical phases, 23−26
Ethical dimension of hybrid
    media events, 127−130

Event, 2, 25, 29, 51, 54, 66, 70, 79,
    104, 110, 119, 123, 135

Facebook, 22, 23, 32, 36, 49, 66,
    78, 88, 95, 110
    see also Twitter
Fear addressing diverse audiences,
    circulation of, 102−104
Financial times, 86
First-hand eyewitness evidence, 79
Foundation, 14, 26
France 2 (France's largest
    television networks), 109,
    112, 116, 118
Free speech, 1, 70, 74, 84, 87
Free World, 2, 127
Freedom of speech, 3, 127−128
French political establishment, 86
French Republic, 44, 99
    principles, 87
    values of freedom of
        expression, 55
French Revolution, 46, 91
Funerals, 42, 61, 86, 98−101, 104
Fundamentalism, 43, 87, 128

Ghetto Muslims, 34
Global communication
    technology, 15
Global hybrid media events, 17,
    24
Global iconic events, 14
Global media, 1, 3, 29, 51
Global mourning, 37−40
GoPro video camera, 112, 113,
    116
Groupe d'Intervention de la
    Gendarmerie Nationale
    (GIGN), 63, 115
Guardian, The, 50−51, 78, 84−85,
    92, 113, 115

Hara-Kiri magazine, 30
Hashtags, 23, 24, 59–60, 75
    affordances, 72–75
    in Twitter messages, 62
    Twitter's key property, 76
Hepp, Andreas, 13, 14
Hervik, Peter, 29, 34
Hollande, François, 43, 44, 48, 53, 86, 87, 96, 100
Hospitality, 131
Hostage situation, 132
    BFM TV, 110–111
    in Dammartin-en-Goële, 108–109
    Independent, The, 111–112
    media, 109–110
    perpetrators in action on live media, 112
Hostage standoff, 41, 113, 125
Human actors, 57, 60
Hybrid, 5–9
    media environment, 58, 124, 125
    media system, 2, 8, 125
    organizations, 6
Hybrid media event(s), 55, 57, 78, 98, 102, 107, 123, 124, 127
    acceleration, 20–21
    acceleration of circulation in, 119–121
    actors, 17–18
    affect, 20
    affordance, 18–19
    amplifying, 75–76
    analysing hybrid media events on Twitter and Beyond, 21–26
    attention, 19–20
    circulation connecting key elements, 126–127

elements, 16
    social and ethical dimensions, 127–130
    of terrorist violence, 104
    see also Media event(s)
Hybridity, 7, 126
Hybridization, 55, 104–105
    of attention, 55
    of *Charlie Hebdo* media event, 87–88
    of media events, 13–16
    moral responsibility, 121
Hypocrisy, 75, 87

Independent, The (newspaper), 44–45, 48, 87, 94, 111, 114
Innocence of Islam (film), 32
Institutional actors, 70, 124, 131
Interdisciplinary analysis of media and terrorism, 4
    hybrid, 5–9
    media event, 9–13
International Business Times, 102
International communication, 5, 7
Internet revenue model, 2
Interpersonal networks, 13
ISIS/ISIL, 129
Islam, 3, 20, 35, 46, 47, 75, 82, 84, 88, 132, 134
Islamist terrorism, 3–4
Islamophobia, 34, 46, 50, 83, 87, 93, 100, 103

Je ne suis pas Charlie, 60, 100
Je suis Ahmed, 60
    as symbol of public solidarity, 83–85
Je Suis Charlie, 37, 50, 60, 91
    counter-narratives opposing, 99–102
    message, 38–39

momentum, 51–55
in social media, 95–96
'Je suis Juif', 42, 99
Je suis Kouachi, 75
Je suis musulman, 100
Jihad and Death, 128
Journalism, 7–8, 33, 130
Journalists, 17, 21, 30, 41, 64, 77,
      104, 107, 110, 112, 116,
      117, 124, 127, 130
Jyllands-Posten (Danish
      newspaper), 31, 33

Katz, Elihu, 5, 9–12, 54, 92, 123,
      128
Kosher Market Siege, 113
      BMF TV, 114
      broadcasting, 115
      hostage, 113–114
      live broadcasting puts hostages
            in danger, 116
Kouachi attacks, 31
Kouachi, Chérif, 34–36, 72, 103,
      112–114, 118, 128
Kouachi, Saïd, 34–36, 72, 103,
      117, 118, 128
Kraidy, Marwan M., 6, 7, 8, 128,
      129

Latour, Bruno, 6, 17,
      57, 128
Le Journal du Dimanche
      newspaper, 53
Le Nouvel Observateur, 113
Liebes, Tamar, 10, 12, 36, 54, 92,
      112, 120
Live broadcasting, 123
      hostages in danger, 116
      of images and information, 117
Live media
      coverage, 118

events, 123
      see also Digital media
Liveness, 108, 120
      acceleration of circulation in
            hybrid media event,
            119–121
      of event, 116
      France's broadcasting
            watchdog, 117
      hostage situation in
            Dammartin-en-Goële,
            108–113
      Jewish supermarket, 118
      Kosher Market Siege, 113–115

Mainstream media, 24, 36, 77,
      88, 89
Manhunt continues, 40–41
Marche républicaine', 45
Martel, Charles (fascist), 74–75
Media, 7, 112
      anthropology, 5
      disasters, 12
      environment, 4, 5, 127
      ethics, 130–131
      making Merabet ideal victim,
            80–81
      media-related practices, 90
      media-saturated symbolic
            communication, 98
      representations, 77
      rituals intensify sense of
            solidarity in, 91–95
      role in terrorism, 4
      technology, 126
      see also Digital media; Live
            media; Social media
Media event(s), 1, 9–13
      Bête et Méchant' newspaper,
            30–35

condensation of meanings,
43–51
hybridization, 13–16
implicit or explicit criteria, 29
Je Suis Charlie' momentum,
51–55
mythologization of victims,
37–43
remediation in digital media,
35–36
theory, 90, 123
Mediated communication, 14,
128, 131
Mediatization, 14, 100
Mediatized ritualization, 55,
90–91
Memes, 2, 20, 24, 77, 90
Merabet, Ahmed, 27, 36, 38, 43,
54, 55, 68, 78–80, 82,
84–86, 88, 89, 99, 100,
129, 130
Microblogging, 58
Mir, Jordi, 36, 79, 80, 83, 129
Mnemonic schemes of
interpretation, 104, 123
Multi-method, 23, 26
'Murderous ideology', 87
Muslim
countries, 32
identity, 129
perpetrators, 77
politicizing Muslim body, 86
terrorism, 3
World League, 32
Mythologization, 15
counts as victim, 41–43
Manhunt continues, 40–41
News coverage and global
mourning, 37–40
of victims, 37

Narratives, 4, 14–15, 16, 41, 42,
55, 110, 127, 132, 133
counter-narratives, 29, 38,
45–49, 50, 73, 101–104
opposing to 'Je Suis Charlie'
solidarity, 99–102
New York Times, The, 49, 84
New Yorker magazine, 70
News coverage, 37–40
News media, 54, 123, 125
9/11 attacks, 3, 47, 54, 88
Non-human actors, 7, 57, 60

Offline
pilgrimages, 93
rituals, 90
Online
pilgrimages, 93
rituals, 90

Palestinian resistance movement,
48
Paris Match, 80
Paying Tribute, 39, 68
Perpetrators in action on live
media, 112
Political communication, 5, 8
PR disaster, 48
Pre-network media events, 124
Professional media, 2, 25, 58, 70,
88
Pulsar, third-party social media
analytics service, 23

Quran, 75

Radical Islam, 3, 86, 128
Radicalization, 35, 128, 129, 130
Radicalized jihadists, 34, 128, 129
Radicalized perpetrators, 128
Re-contextualization, 10–11

Remediation, 15, 29
  in digital media, 35–36
  of messages, 119
Republican March(es), 45, 94
Rest in Peace (RIP), 39
Ritual(s), 90
  digital rituals, 92, 100
  intensify sense of solidarity in
    media, 91–95
  pilgrimage, 93
  practices, 95, 104–105
  ritualization, 97, 106
Roncin, Joachim, 37, 38, 61, 93
Roy, Olivier, 35, 132, 133
Roy's analysis, 128

Salafism, 128
School shooters, 129
Silverstone, Roger, 135
Sincerity, 131, 132
Social acceleration, 21
Social media, 2, 54, 88, 89, 123,
    125
  algorithms, 4
  culture, 82
  giants, 63
  Je Suis Charlie' in, 95–96
  see also Digital media; Live
    media
Social network analytics approach
    (SNA approach),
    23, 63
Social networking sites, 1, 10, 14,
    42, 104
Social theory, 5, 130
Solidarity, 87
  huge show of solidarity in Paris
    against terrorism, 49–51
  rituals intensify sense of, 91–95
Sonnevend, Julia, 14, 15, 16, 26,
    38, 50, 51, 54

Streaming, 107, 108, 110, 116, 123
Stylist Magazine, 37, 61

Telegraph, The, 45–46, 94–95, 97
Terror attacks, 89
Terrorism, 2–3, 43, 127, 132
  huge show of solidarity in Paris
    against, 49–51
  towarding interdisciplinary
    analysis of media and,
    4–13
Terrorist
  action, 128
  attack, 127
  organizations, 129
  violence, 128
Terrorist violence, hybrid media
    events of
  analysing hybrid media events
    on Twitter and Beyond,
    21–26
  Charlie Hebdo attacks, 1–4
  elements of hybrid media
    events, 16–21
  hybridization of media events,
    13–16
  interdisciplinary analysis of
    media and terrorism, 4–13
  structure of book, 26–27
Texts, 2, 19, 20, 90
*TF*1 (France's largest television
    networks), 112, 118
Tracing @JeSuisKouachi, 72–75
Transcultural phenomena, 13–14
Transculturalism, 8–9
Translocal phenomena, 13–14
Transnational phenomena, 13–14
Tribute, 49, 68, 69, 85, 92, 95, 97,
    100
Tweets, 23, 59, 60, 65, 73, 90
Twitter, 57, 59, 64, 65, 95

actors, 63, 64–65
analysing hybrid media events
    on Twitter and Beyond, 21
Charlie Hebdo anatomy attacks
    on, 60–61
dynamics, 65–72
empirical phases, 23–26
hashtags in Twitter messages
    posted on *Charlie Hebdo*
    attacks, 62

Union of French Islamic
    Organisations (UOIF), 32

Victims
    ideal victim, 81–82, 86, 89
    mythologization of, 37–43
Video material, 115
Videos, 20, 24, 90, 91, 115

Vigipirate Plan on 'attack' level,
    43–44
Violence, 10, 39
Violent action, 128, 129
Violent global media events, 121
Violent media events, 13, 41, 123
Violent terrorist occurrence, 89

Wagner-Pacifici, Robin, 54
'Western' victims, 77
World political elites, 43–45
World Trade Center, 3

Xenophobia, 87

YouTube, 23, 63, 69

Zelizer, Barbie, 106